# SCREAMING SKULLS

*Other Avon Camelot Books by*
**Daniel Cohen**

THE MUMMY'S CURSE:
101 OF THE WORLD'S STRANGEST MYSTERIES

Avon Books are available at special quantity discounts for bulk purchases for sales promotions, premiums, fund raising or educational use. Special books, or book excerpts, can also be created to fit specific needs.

For details write or telephone the office of the Director of Special Markets, Avon Books, Dept. FP, 1350 Avenue of the Americas, New York, New York 10019, 1-800-238-0658.

# SCREAMING SKULLS

## 101 OF THE WORLD'S GREATEST GHOST STORIES

# DANIEL COHEN

AN AVON CAMELOT BOOK

> **VISIT OUR WEBSITE AT**
> **http://AvonBooks.com**

SCREAMING SKULLS is an original publication of Avon Books. This work has never before appeared in book form.

AVON BOOKS
A division of
The Hearst Corporation
1350 Avenue of the Americas
New York, New York 10019

Copyright © 1996 by Daniel Cohen
Published by arrangement with the author
Library of Congress Catalog Card Number: 96-6280
ISBN: 0-380-78349-5
RL: 4.9

All rights reserved, which includes the right to reproduce this book or portions thereof in any form whatsoever except as provided by the U.S. Copyright Law. For information address Henry Morrison, Inc., 320 McLean Street, Bedford Hills, New York 10507.

Library of Congress Cataloging in Publication Data:

Cohen, Daniel, 1936–
  Screaming skulls: 101 of the world's greatest ghost stories/Daniel Cohen.
    p.    cm.—(Avon Camelot book)
  Summary: A collection of stories covering a wide spectrum from poltergeist cases that have been carefully investigated to legends and ghostly folklore.
  1. Ghosts—Juvenile literature. 2. Haunted houses—Juvenile literature. [1. Ghosts. 2. Haunted houses.] I. Title.
BF1461.C662   1996                                                96-6280
133.1—dc20                                                            CIP
                                                                       AC

First Avon Camelot Printing: July 1996

CAMELOT TRADEMARK REG. U.S. PAT. OFF. AND IN OTHER COUNTRIES, MARCA REGISTRADA, HECHO EN U.S.A.

Printed in the U.S.A.

OPM   10  9  8  7  6  5  4  3  2  1

> If you purchased this book without a cover, you should be aware that this book is stolen property. It was reported as "unsold and destroyed" to the publisher, and neither the author nor the publisher has received any payment for this "stripped book."

# CONTENTS

### INTRODUCTION: Do You Believe in Ghosts?

## PART 1  FAMOUS GHOSTS

| | | |
|---|---|---|
| 1 | The Oldest Ghost Story | 5 |
| 2 | The Emperor's Ghost | 6 |
| 3 | Aaron Burr and His Daughter | 7 |
| 4 | Pearlin Jean | 9 |
| 5 | A Royal Murder? | 11 |
| 6 | The Man in Grey | 13 |
| 7 | Poe's Troubled Spirit | 14 |
| 8 | A Hero's Ghost | 16 |
| 9 | Abraham Lincoln's Ghost | 18 |
| 10 | Lincoln's Assassins | 20 |
| 11 | The Admiral Returns | 21 |
| 12 | Katie King | 23 |
| 13 | The Return of Marie Laveau | 26 |
| 14 | Patience Worth | 28 |
| 15 | Harry Houdini | 29 |
| 16 | Walter the Guide | 32 |
| 17 | Rosalie | 34 |

| 18 | The Ghost Hunter's Ghost | 36 |
| 19 | Elvis | 38 |

## PART II  HAUNTED PLACES

| 20 | A Prehistoric Ghost | 43 |
| 21 | Haunted Battlefields | 44 |
| 22 | The Samurai Ghosts | 47 |
| 23 | The Bloody Tower | 48 |
| 24 | The Green Ghost of Vauvert | 50 |
| 25 | The Ghostly Monks of Glastonbury | 51 |
| 26 | Grim Glamis Castle | 53 |
| 27 | Haunted Hampton Court | 55 |
| 28 | The Calvados Haunting | 57 |
| 29 | The Hoby Ghosts | 58 |
| 30 | The Weir House | 60 |
| 31 | The Brown Lady | 62 |
| 32 | The Cock Lane Ghost | 65 |
| 33 | The Hydesville Haunting | 67 |
| 34 | The Octagon | 69 |
| 35 | The Cheltenham Haunting | 71 |
| 36 | The *Great Eastern* | 73 |
| 37 | *Grief* | 76 |
| 38 | The Abandoned Lighthouse | 78 |
| 39 | The Berkeley Square Horror | 80 |
| 40 | The Winchester Mystery House | 82 |
| 41 | The Haunted U-boat | 85 |
| 42 | Borley Rectory | 87 |
| 43 | Deadly Crossings | 89 |
| 44 | Roadside Phantoms | 91 |

## PART III   ANIMAL PHANTOMS

| | | |
|---|---|---|
| 45 | Phantom Dogs | 95 |
| 46 | The White Rabbit of Crank | 96 |
| 47 | The Ghost Steer | 99 |
| 48 | The Demon Cat of Washington | 101 |
| 49 | The Werewolf's Ghost | 102 |
| 50 | The Bird of Lincoln's Inn | 104 |
| 51 | Terhune's Ghost Dog | 106 |

## PART IV   POLTERGEISTS

| | | |
|---|---|---|
| 52 | The Drummer of Tedworth | 111 |
| 53 | The Epworth Poltergeist | 113 |
| 54 | The Bell Witch | 115 |
| 55 | The Fiery Poltergeist | 118 |

## PART V   WARNINGS AND APPARITIONS

| | | |
|---|---|---|
| 56 | The Spirit of Samuel | 123 |
| 57 | The Black Velvet Ribbon | 124 |
| 58 | The Radiant Boys | 127 |
| 59 | The River Ghost | 129 |
| 60 | Lord Lyttelton's Doom | 130 |
| 61 | Mark Twain's Vision | 131 |
| 62 | Lieutenant Sutton's Return | 134 |
| 63 | The White Lady of the Old Palace | 136 |
| 64 | Death Foreseen | 137 |
| 65 | The Appearance of Lieutenant McConnell | 139 |
| 66 | Commander Potter's Vision | 141 |
| 67 | "Beware Jack" | 143 |

## PART VI  GHOSTLY PHENOMENA

| | | |
|---|---|---|
| 68 | China's Walking Corpses | 147 |
| 69 | The *Palatine* Light | 148 |
| 70 | The Screaming Woman | 149 |
| 71 | The Versailles Adventure | 150 |
| 72 | Screaming Skulls | 153 |
| 73 | Corder's Skull | 155 |
| 74 | Ghostly Footsteps | 157 |
| 75 | Summoning a Spirit | 158 |
| 76 | Spook Lights | 160 |
| 77 | The Ouija Board | 161 |
| 78 | Buried Alive | 163 |
| 79 | The Phantom Faces | 164 |
| 80 | Black Aggie | 166 |
| 81 | The Phantom Bus | 167 |
| 82 | The Hairy Hands | 168 |
| 83 | The Return Flight | 170 |
| 84 | The Tulip Staircase | 172 |
| 85 | Phone Call from the Dead | 173 |
| 86 | Hitchcock's Favorite Ghost Story | 175 |

## PART VII  GHOSTLY LEGENDS

| | | |
|---|---|---|
| 87 | Ghosts of the Ancient Greeks | 179 |
| 88 | The *Flying Dutchman* | 180 |
| 89 | The Demon Lover | 182 |
| 90 | The Ghostly Wanderer | 184 |
| 91 | Tregagle | 186 |
| 92 | Lady Howard | 187 |
| 93 | Christmas Ghosts | 189 |

| | | |
|---|---|---|
| 94 | The Phantom Brakeman | 192 |
| 95 | The Phantom Hitchhiker | 194 |
| 96 | Ride with the Dead | 196 |
| 97 | The Death Car | 197 |
| 98 | The Angels of Mons | 200 |
| 99 | The Ghostly Truck Driver | 201 |
| 100 | A Vietnam War Ghost | 203 |
| 101 | "I'm Goin' Home" | 204 |

# SCREAMING SKULLS

# INTRODUCTION: DO YOU BELIEVE IN GHOSTS?

If you believe in ghosts, and even if you don't, you are probably fascinated by them. You have to be a pretty dull brick if you're not.

Ghosts stories have been popular at every time in history and with every culture. You must have spent more than one evening sitting around in the near darkness with a group of friends terrifying one another by exchanging ghost stories. Maybe you didn't really believe the stories you heard. Maybe you didn't even believe the stories you told. But you sure found it hard to go to sleep that night. And every noise sounded as if it came from beyond the grave.

Thousands of years ago prehistoric hunters, sitting around a fire at the mouth of a cave, probably scared one another with stories not so very different from the ones that you and your friends exchanged.

I have spent a large part of my professional life with ghosts—well, not exactly with them—but writing about them. I have, in one way or another, encountered thousands of ghost stories. Here are 101 of my favorites.

The ghosts that you are about to meet cover a wide spectrum, from poltergeist cases that have been carefully investigated to legends and ghostly folklore. There are very ancient ghosts—a horseman from the Stone Age is probably the oldest—and modern ones, like a ghost from the Vietnam War.

What is it about these stories that we find so appealing? Lord Halifax was a celebrated collector of ghostly accounts, and his collection is one of the best. His son tried to explain the fascination that such tales held for his father. "They appealed to his natural sense of mystery and romance." But there was more.

"And I cannot doubt that the true secret of the appeal made to his thought by the mysterious or so-called uncanny was the glimpse that such narratives or events might seem to afford to the hidden realities of the unseen world."

That says it nicely—romance, mystery, and the possibility of a peek into the unknown. What else can you want?

# I. Famous Ghosts

# THE OLDEST GHOST STORY

What may be the oldest surviving "true" ghost story comes from the pen of Pliny the Younger, who lived in Rome in the first century A.D. It contains many of the elements that can be found in later ghostly accounts.

In a letter Pliny wrote of a large house in Athens that had acquired the reputation of being haunted. People told of horrible noises, like groans and the clanking of chains, followed by the appearance of the phantom of an old man in chains. A few skeptics who had decided to spend a night in the house were nearly frightened out of their wits and died shortly after their experience.

One day the philosopher Athenodorus came to Athens looking for a place to live. He asked how much it would cost to rent the vacant house, and when the figure he was given seemed remarkably low, he inquired why and was told the whole story of the haunting. The philosopher decided to take the house anyway.

On his first night Athenodorus was sitting up late working on a particularly difficult problem, which fully absorbed his attention. When the groans and the clanking chains began he was not disturbed. It was not until the phantom stood right in front of him that the philosopher even bothered to look up.

It was exactly as it had been described, and it seemed to beckon to him. At first he indicated that he was too busy, but when the ghost became insistent he decided to follow it.

The ghost led the philosopher into the garden and pointed at a spot in the shrubbery. Then it disappeared. Athenodorus marked the spot, then went back to the house and fell asleep. The next morning he went to the magistrates, and suggested that the spot the ghost had indicated should be investigated.

This was done, and when the investigators began to dig they found a human skeleton just a few feet below the surface. Ancient and rusted chains still clung to the bones. The remains were carefully collected and properly buried. The house was then cleansed with various rituals, and after that it was never again troubled by ghosts or bad luck.

# THE EMPEROR'S GHOST

The Roman Emperor Nero has an absolutely vile reputation. He persecuted the Christians, and he allegedly instigated the burning of Rome. His personal excesses and extravagances finally turned the aristocrats and the army of Rome against him. Pressed on all sides by his enemies, Nero killed himself in A.D. 68 at the place where the church of Santa Maria del Popolo now stands.

According to legend a magnificent walnut tree sprang up on the spot where Nero's remains were buried. After his death the emperor's ghost and other evil spirits reportedly haunted the place where he was buried and tormented any citizen who happened to wander by.

The situation grew so bad that in 1099 the people of Rome requested the help of Pope Paschal II. In response he prescribed three days of prayer and fasting. It was said that during that time a vision of the Virgin Mary appeared to the pope and directed that on the third Sunday after the fasting period, he was to cut down the walnut tree and dig up the emperor's remains. Then both the tree and the remains were to be burned and thrown in the Tiber River. The pope carried out these instructions, and Nero's ghost troubled the area no more.

Soon after the exorcism, by popular request, a chapel was built where the walnut tree had stood. In 1472, Pope Sixtus V replaced the little church with Santa Maria del Popolo, a majestic building that was later modified by the great sculptor and architect Giovanni Lorenzo Bernini. Reliefs on the basilica's ceiling commemorate the conquest of the wicked ghost of Nero.

# AARON BURR AND HIS DAUGHTER

Aaron Burr was one of the most colorful and controversial characters in American history. His ghost has occasionally been reported in lower Manhattan, where he spent much of his life. But even more famous are the ghosts of many of those associated with Burr.

After the American Revolution Burr was very nearly

elected president of the United States, losing a close vote in the House of Representatives to Thomas Jefferson. Direct election of presidents as we have now had not yet become a part of the U.S. political system. Burr was made vice president. But he always harbored a grudge against Alexander Hamilton, who he thought had cost him the presidency. Hamilton hated Burr as well.

The political quarrel ended in a duel between Hamilton and Burr in Weehawken, New Jersey, on July 11, 1804. Hamilton was fatally wounded and taken back to New York, where he died a few days later. Hamilton's ghost has often been reported in the Greenwich Village area where he died.

Burr was forced to flee New York because dueling was illegal, and because of the enmity of Hamilton's friends. After many adventures he was accused of treason and had to flee the country entirely. The only person in the world he really cared about was his beautiful daughter Theodosia. She pleaded with her father to return to America. Finally, in 1814 he decided to do so. Theodosia was to take a ship from the South, where she lived, to New York, where her father was going to land. The ship carrying her never arrived. It is believed to have sunk during a storm off Cape Hatteras, North Carolina, where the ghost of Theodosia Burr has regularly been reported walking the beach.

Aaron Burr stayed in New York and became a successful lawyer. In 1833, when he was seventy-seven, he married a wealthy widow, Eliza Jumel, who was about twenty years his junior. She had a reputation of her own—she was rumored to have killed her first husband for his money. The second marriage didn't last. Within a year Eliza sued for divorce. She accused Burr of running around with other women, and though Aaron Burr was then seventy-eight, the charge may well have been true.

The divorce was granted just a few days before Burr's death.

Eliza Jumel lived on until 1865. She died in the grand Jumel Mansion at the age of ninety-three. The mansion still stands and is an historic site preserved by the city of New York. Children in the area say that occasionally an old woman comes out on the balcony to chase them away. Since no old woman lives in the mansion now, the figure is assumed to be the ghost of Eliza Jumel.

# PEARLIN JEAN

The mansion of Allanbank at Edrom in Berwickshire, Scotland, was haunted by a strange female figure whose head and shoulders were covered with blood. This was the ghost called Pearlin Jean. Pearlin is a fine lace which was on the dress the ghostly figure wore.

In the seventeenth century Allanbank was owned by the Stuart family. Sometime around 1670 Sir Robert Stuart was in France, where he took up with a lovely young French girl named Jeanne de la Salle. She fell hopelessly in love with the Scottish nobleman. But for him it was merely a passing affair. He knew that there was no way he would be able to take Jeanne back to Scotland and have her accepted by his family.

So one day Sir Robert just got into his carriage and started to drive away. The poor girl ran after the carriage and tried to climb in, but Sir Robert ordered his driver not to stop. Jeanne was thrown to the ground and the heavy wheels of the carriage passed over her head.

By the time he got back to Scotland the heartless Sir Robert had almost forgotten the incident. But as he drove up to Allanbank he saw the figure of the dead Jeanne sitting on the archway high above the entrance, gazing down at him with her crushed and bloody head.

The homecoming celebrations were canceled. Sir Robert was no longer the confident and carefree young man who had driven up to the gates of Allanbank. And he was not the only one to see the apparition. Footsteps and the mysterious rustling of a lace dress were heard throughout the house, particularly at night. Doors opened and shut suddenly, and there were horrifying screams. From time to time a servant would come around a corner, and there she would be!

In 1697 Sir Robert married. His wife was a woman of exceptionally calm and stable temperament. She knew about the ghost—everybody in Scotland knew about Pearlin Jean by that time. But since no one had ever actually been harmed, she regarded the ghost as more of a nuisance than a real threat, and refused to be bothered by it.

However, when Sir Robert had a portrait of his wife hung in the family portrait gallery next to his own this provoked an outburst of unprecedented fury on the part of Pearlin Jean. The nearly frantic Sir Robert called in seven ministers from the Church of Scotland to exorcise the ghost. The solemn ceremonies had no effect at all.

Then Sir Robert had a macabre idea. He recalled that Jeanne de la Salle had said before she died that she would "come between" him and any woman he would marry. So he had a portrait of Jeanne painted and hung the new picture between his own and that of his wife. Amazingly, the trick worked, at least for a while.

Eventually the ghost of Pearlin Jean came to be regarded almost with affection by the servants of Allenbank, and each had a favorite story to tell of an encounter with the ghost.

If adults had ceased to take Pearlin Jean seriously, the same cannot be said for children. Generations of children who grew up in the vicinity of Allanbank were terrified by stories of the ghost. "If you aren't good," they were told, "the bloodstained ghost of Pearlin Jean will get you."

# A ROYAL MURDER?

One of the royal residences in London, St. James Palace, is supposed to be haunted by a "horrible ghost." It is the specter of a small man, his throat slit from ear to ear, sitting up in a bed with his head propped precariously against the wall and his body and the bedclothes drenched with blood.

This ghost is supposed to have had its origin in a murder that took place on May 31, 1810. The palace was primary residence of the dreadful duke of Cumberland, the worst of King George III's children. He returned home late that night and shouts and the sound of a fight were heard coming from his rooms. The servants simply assumed the duke was drunk, as usual, and took no action.

Cumberland had two valets, Yew and Sellis, and

about an hour after his return the duke called for Yew. The valet found his master standing in his room, his shirtfront covered with blood, and his bloodstained sword on the floor. The duke said that he had been attacked and wounded and he asked the valet to send for his doctor. The doctor arrived within minutes and found that the duke was in no danger. His only wound was a deep cut on his sword hand.

Almost two hours had passed since Cumberland had returned to the palace and now, with the wound dressed and the room rearranged, the duke said to Yew, "Call Sellis." Yew went to Sellis's room and found him in his bed his head raised against the headboard—and nearly severed from his neck. A blood-covered razor was found on the other side of the room.

At the inquest Cumberland said that Sellis had tried to murder him and then committed suicide. This was an improbable explanation. The razor was too far from Sellis's body to have been thrown there by a man who had just cut his own throat. That the valet, a small man, would have attacked the burly duke in the first place seems unlikely. A more probable explanation is that the duke had an affair with Sellis's daughter, who then either had a child or killed herself. In order to silence Sellis the duke cut the valet's throat with his sword. Then he had probably gashed himself with a razor, to make it appear that there had been a fight.

Cumberland was not prosecuted, of course, but he had never been popular, and he was now openly booed in the streets of London, and was never able to attend public functions again.

# THE MAN IN GREY

The most famous of London's many theater ghosts is the Man in Grey who haunts the venerable Theatre Royal in Drury Lane. The ghost has been described as looking like an eighteenth century dandy. He wears a white wig, a three-cornered hat, a sword, and riding boots. The most obvious part of his attire is the grey cloak he wears over his shoulder, and it is this that has given him the name, the Man in Grey.

The Man in Grey generally appears in the audience area of the theater between the hours of 9:00 A.M. and 6:00 P.M., before the curtain call of the evening performance. The figure takes a slow and stately walk from one end of the balcony to the opposite wall, where he disappears. If anyone approaches too closely, the ghost will disappear.

King George VI once went to a matinee at the theater specifically to see the ghost. But the spirit apparently did not obey a royal command and failed to let himself be seen. It is believed that many sightings of the Man in Grey go unreported because people who see him, and have not heard the legend, simply assume that he is an actor in costume.

No one is sure whose ghost this is. The popular legend is that he was a young man who fell in love with one of the theater actresses. In a jealous rage the girl's lover killed the man and hid his body somewhere behind the walls of the theater. There are rumors that a man's skeleton, with a dagger between its ribs and shreds of a grey cloak still clinging to it was found behind one of the theater walls by workmen during a renovation, but the story has proved impossible to confirm.

Despite this rather gruesome history, the ghost is regarded with great affection by those who have performed at the Theatre Royal. It is believed that if he appears before the opening of a new show, then the production is sure to be a success. Perhaps the ghost is not interested in attending flops.

An offer to exorcise the ghost was turned down by the theater management. Why chase away an attraction like that?

# POE'S TROUBLED SPIRIT

Edgar Allan Poe is America's foremost writer of tales of terror. Poe never actually wrote a ghost story, though most people think he did. However, his stories are macabre enough, and coupled with his own troubled life and mysterious death, he has inspired ghostly tales.

In late September 1849, Poe, who had been living in Richmond, Virginia, traveled up to Baltimore, Maryland, where he had also lived. According to one account, he attended a birthday party in Baltimore, took one glass of wine for a toast, left the party, and disappeared.

The next five days are a complete blank. On October 3 he was found wandering the streets mumbling incoherently. He was also wearing someone else's ill-fitting clothes. Poe was taken to the Church Home Hospital in Baltimore, where he died without ever regaining his senses. He was never able to tell people what had happened.

Some people believed that Poe was an alcoholic. He certainly had a "drinking problem," but it may have been due to an inborn inability to tolerate even small amounts of alcohol. The most obvious explanation for his disappearance is that he just got drunk and wandered off.

There is another story that about a year before his death he was diagnosed as having some sort of brain injury, and that he did not have long to live. A more exotic explanation has to do with the election that was being held in Baltimore at the time of Poe's disappearance. It was said that a drunken or drugged Poe was dragged from one polling place to another so that he could vote many times.

We must resign ourselves to the fact that we will never know what happened to one of America's greatest and most influential writers.

Poe was buried behind the Westminster Presbyterian Church in Baltimore. There is a marker which commemorates the spot. Later his remains were moved to the Poe family plot in the same churchyard.

Those are the known facts. Now the ghost. The figure of a man dressed in black, early nineteenth century clothes, has been seen staggering through the streets of the old section of Baltimore, much as Poe might have done during his final, fatal days. The same figure has been reported in the corridors of the hospital where he died.

Visitors have reported the spectral figure of Poe in

the Westminster Presbyterian churchyard, both near his original grave and his final resting place.

But most of the ghostly reports come from the Poe House in Baltimore. Poe lived in many different places, but for several years lived with his relatives in a small house at 203 North Amity Street. The house has been restored as an historical monument and museum to commemorate the writer.

A large number of visitors have reported sensing the presence of the ghost, and a few have said they actually saw a ghostly figure. The reputation of the Poe House for being haunted is so strong, it is said that the street gangs which abound in this poor and run-down neighborhood just stay away from it.

Then there is the mysterious person, dressed in black, who every January 19, the anniversary of Poe's death, places a bunch of roses and a bottle of brandy on the writer's grave.

# A HERO'S GHOST

Stephen Decatur was one of America's greatest naval heroes. Handsome, charming, and fiercely patriotic, he was idolized during the early 1800s. He was the man who popularized the saying, "My country right or wrong."

But Decatur had a deadly enemy, another American naval man named James Barron. Decatur had been one of the members of a board which had suspended Barron from the navy for failing to resist a British boarding party during the War of 1812.

As Decatur's career advanced and he became more and more famous, Barron came to blame him, and him alone, for his misfortunes. Forgotten and embittered, James Barron plotted his revenge.

He started a campaign to provoke Decatur into a duel. Dueling was illegal, though it went on anyway. When he was young Decatur had fought several duels. Dueling was excused in young men who were considered "hot-blooded." But Stephen Decatur was now a mature man. He was not anxious to fight another duel. Finally he was goaded into accepting the challenge. He wrote ". . . if we fight, it must be on your own seeking."

The night before the duel Decatur spent much of the time gazing gloomily out of the window of his Washington, D.C., home. Even if he survived, he knew that his reputation must suffer. He also had a premonition of how the duel would turn out.

Before sunrise of March 14, 1820, Decatur slipped out a back door of his house carrying a box containing his dueling pistols. He never told his young wife what he was going to do. He rode to a field near Bladensburg, Maryland. The place was a notorious dueling ground. A brook that ran nearby had been christened Blood Run.

The duel was to be fought at a mere eight paces—murderously close. It was meant to be a duel to the death. At the count of two, two shots rang out. Barron immediately fell, wounded in the hip. Decatur stood for a moment. Then he dropped his smoking gun, clutched his right side, and fell. He had been mortally wounded.

Despite the manner of his death the country mourned its hero. Flags flew at half-staff, and towns all over the country were named after him.

About a year after Decatur's death people reported seeing his ghost standing at the window of the room that had been his bedroom. The spirit appeared to be doing just what Decatur himself had been doing the night before the fatal duel—staring morosely.

In order to stop the stories, the window was boarded up. But people passing the house, which still stands on Lafayette Square, report that they have seen the semi-transparent form of the naval hero at the boarded-up window.

Some people have also reported that early some mornings they have seen his ghostly form slipping out of the back door. The figure carries a black box under its arm. Decatur would have carried his dueling pistols in just such a box.

# ABRAHAM LINCOLN'S GHOST

Of all America's ghosts, that of the martyred president Abraham Lincoln is undoubtedly the most famous. After his assassination in 1865, sightings of Lincoln's ghost were reported from the White House, in Washington, D.C., to Lincoln's tomb in Springfield, Illinois, where his body is buried.

The White House sightings are the best-known. Once the ghost was seen by a queen. Shortly after the end of World War II, Queen Wilhelmina of the Netherlands was a guest at the White House. Late one night she heard a knock at her door. She assumed that it must be something important. But when she opened the door she saw a tall bearded figure, all dressed in black with a shawl draped around his shoulders. She knew who it was, and she fainted.

Eleanor Roosevelt, who lived in the White House as first lady longer than anyone else, never claimed to have seen the ghost herself. But she often told the story of the experience of one of her staff members. Her secretary was passing the Lincoln bedroom and saw a familiar-looking figure sitting on the bed pulling on his boots. The Lincoln bedroom was used as a guest room for visiting heads of state, but the secretary knew that there were no guests in the room at that time. On another occasion President Franklin D. Roosevelt's valet apparently ran out of the White House shouting that he had seen Lincoln's ghost.

Many who did not actually see the ghost said they felt its presence. Winston Churchill, Britain's prime minister during World War II, never admitted seeing or feeling any spirit. But he hated sleeping in the Lincoln bedroom. Sometimes White House servants would find that Churchill had moved out of the bedroom in the middle of the night and was sleeping in a room across the hall. He never explained why he acted this way.

In life Lincoln was a melancholy man whose life had often been touched by tragedy. His favorite son, twelve-year-old Willie, died halfway through Lincoln's first term in office. The death deeply affected Lincoln and nearly shattered his wife Mary. The death gave her a fascination with spiritualism, and séances were held in the White House, though it is not clear if Lincoln himself ever attended one. Willie's ghost has been sighted around the White House on several occasions.

The night before the assassination Lincoln is said to

have dreamed of his own death. And after his death many spirit mediums claimed to be in contact with the dead president.

# LINCOLN'S ASSASSINS

The assassination of Abraham Lincoln seems almost entirely enveloped in a ghostly fog. Not only have numerous sightings of the murdered president been reported, those who planned and carried out the assassination also do not seem to rest easy in their graves.

The assassination plot was hatched by a group of Southern sympathizers headed by the actor John Wilkes Booth. The plotters met at a Washington boardinghouse owned by Mary Surratt. Her son John was one of the conspirators. Whether Mrs. Surratt herself was part of the plot is less clear, but she was arrested, tried, and hanged with the others.

For years those who rented the old boardinghouse said that they could hear "mumblings" and "muffled sounds" as if a group of men were talking in low voices. Some said that could actually hear the details of the assassination being plotted.

The same sort of sounds have been reported at the tavern once owned by the Surratt family in Maryland. Mary Surratt's ghost had been seen there and at a barred window in the Old Brick Capital, a building that was used as a prison during the Civil War. The building no longer exists. It was torn down to make room for the U.S. Supreme Court building.

After Booth shot Lincoln at Ford's Theater, he jumped from the box in which the president had been sitting onto the stage to make his escape. There is an enduring legend that any actor or actress who attempts to speak his or her lines along the route across the stage where Booth made his escape will become hopelessly muddled. Ghostly footsteps, rumored to be Booth's, are also heard in the theater.

# THE ADMIRAL RETURNS

Two great mysteries surround the life and death of Admiral Sir George Tryon. First, he committed one of the greatest and deadliest blunders in all naval history. And no one knows why.

Second, after the disaster, as his body lay at the bottom of the Mediterranean, Admiral Tryon's ghost appeared at a reception his wife was giving at their home in London. And no one knows why—or how.

On June 22, 1893, Admiral Tryon was commanding the British fleet in the Mediterranean. He was conducting maneuvers off the coast of Tripoli in North Africa. There were eleven ships in the fleet. The admiral was aboard his flagship the HMS *Victoria*.

He ordered the ships to form two parallel lines. One

line was headed by the *Victoria*, the other by the battleship HMS *Camperdown* under the command of Rear Admiral Albert Markham. The two lines were then ordered to turn inward, toward one another.

This was a standard maneuver, and it was perfectly safe, if the ships were not too close to one another. But the ships were too close, and if the lines turned inward the lead ships, *Victoria* and *Camperdown*, would collide. Everyone in the fleet seemed to know this except Admiral Tryon. Unfortunately, no one had the courage to tell the admiral that his order was insane, or even to question the wisdom of what was being done. Admiral Markham hesitated but from the *Victoria* came the message, "What are you waiting for?" So the *Camperdown* made the turn and steamed ahead.

When the ships were only two hundred yards apart Markham ordered his ship to stop and reverse engines. Admiral Tryon, too, seems to have realized that something was terribly wrong and gave the same order. It was too late. The *Camperdown*, which had a steel ram in her bow, tore into the *Victoria*.

Water poured in through the gash. Within minutes she began to sink. Some 355 of the 600 officers and men aboard the *Victoria* died in the disaster. In the best tradition of the British navy, Admiral Tryon went down with his ship, and never had to explain why he made this deadly error. Shortly before he disappeared he was heard to mutter, to no one in particular, "It was all my fault, entirely my fault."

At about the time that the *Victoria* was sinking off the African coast, Lady Tryon was giving a reception in the couple's elegant house in Eaton Square, London. A portly figure in an admiral's uniform came down the main staircase and began greeting some of the guests by name. The guests recognized the figure as that of Admiral Sir George Tryon.

Lady Tryon herself never saw the figure, and assured the guests that it could not possibly be her husband because he was commanding the fleet in the Mediterranean. What she did not know, and what no one in England knew until the following day, was that Admiral Tryon, and many under his command, lay dead on the floor of the sea.

# KATIE KING

Katie King is the ghost of a person who may never have existed. She comes from a large family of ghosts. They first made their appearance in 1852 in a log cabin in Athens County, Ohio. The cabin was owned by Jonathan Koons, who said he was a spiritualist medium, and his cabin was the scene of many lively séances.

The first to appear was John King, patriarch of the clan. In life he was supposed to have been a pirate, and his language at the séances was colorful and often salty. In addition to the old pirate there were some fifty-six other Kings who showed up at Koons's séances. Most had little or no personality and soon returned to the world from which they were supposed to have come, without leaving a trace. Daughter Katie was different. She began to appear at the séances of other spiritualist mediums. This was not unusual. Celebrated spirit guides, be they the spirits of famous people or of individuals who may or may not have existed, were often used by different mediums, just as celebrities today make the rounds of many different talk shows.

Katie became a true ghostly star through her association with the young English medium Florence Cook. Cook was one of the first mediums to produce materializations of the entire human body in the light—or in the half-light of a gaslit séance room. The medium would sit in a dark-curtained recess of the room—called the cabinet—while she was in a trance state. After a while a white-garbed figure calling herself Katie King would emerge from the cabinet.

During the tests the medium was sometimes tied to her chair, and there were other elementary controls. But skeptics insisted that Cook could easily have slipped out of the ropes, and that the "spirit" of Katie King was really Florence Cook in a sheet. Indeed photos of the medium and the spirit show that they looked exactly alike.

The trickery seemed so obvious that it would probably be entirely forgotten today if the ghostly phenomenon had not been investigated by Sir William Crookes. Crookes was a physicist, developer of the device that made possible the X-ray. He was also elected president of the Royal Society, the most eminent scientific society in the world at that time. He was a force to be reckoned with in nineteenth century science.

Starting in 1874, Crookes held a series of séances with Florence Cook. The major charge brought against the medium was that, like Clark Kent and Superman, Florence and Katie were never seen together. But Crookes insisted that he had often seen the medium and the spirit together, and that they were two separate beings.

*Florence Cook (top) and her spirit "Katie" (bottom). Notice the striking resemblance?*

Crookes himself was photographed walking arm and arm with the spirit. He wrote, "It was a common thing for seven or eight of us in the laboratory to see Miss Cook and Katie at the same time under the full blaze of an electric light." There was even supposed to be a photo of Katie and Florence Cook together, but this does not appear to have survived.

There are three possible explanations for this extraordinary series of events. First that Florence Cook was a fraud and one of the world's most eminent scientists was a deluded fool. The second is that the world famous scientist was not a dupe but an active participant in one of the most flagrant hoaxes in history.

The third possibility, of course, is that Katie King really was a ghost.

# THE RETURN OF MARIE LAVEAU

The city of New Orleans has always been associated with voodoo. And of all the voodoo practitioners the most celebrated, and most mysterious, was the woman called Marie Laveau. No one knows who she really was, where she came from, how old she was when she died—or if she really died at all. But there is no doubt that there was at least one person who called herself Marie Laveau.

She was first heard of presiding over voodoo ceremonies in a place in New Orleans called Congo Square in the 1830s. From her little house on St. Anne Street she sold powerful magical charms and potions. Her customers ranged from slaves to members of some of New Orleans' leading families. They would come to St. Anne Street at night to buy potions that would help them find a lover, or get rid of one.

Fifty years later Marie was still holding voodoo ceremonies and selling charms at the St. Anne Street house. Witnesses said that she didn't look a day older than she had in the 1830s. She disappeared after a terrible hurricane struck New Orleans in the 1890s. According to some legends Marie was protected by her magic and couldn't be killed. She simply left New Orleans for her own mysterious reasons. Others say she changed herself into a crow or some other animal.

Some historians believe that there were really two Marie Laveaus. The original Marie died around 1881; after that another woman, perhaps her daughter, continued practicing voodoo for another ten years or so under the same name.

At the old St. Louis Cemetery in New Orleans there are two unmarked tombs associated with Marie Laveau. It is believed that the original Marie is buried in one of them, though no one knows which one. Even today people leave voodoo offerings on the tombs.

There are also regular reports that Marie's ghost has been seen in the vicinity of the cemetery. One person said that the ghost became indignant when he didn't recognize her and hit him across the face.

The site of Marie's old house at 1020 St. Anne Street is also supposed to be haunted by the ghosts of the voodoo queen and her followers, who can still be heard performing their rituals from beyond the grave.

# PATIENCE WORTH

The most prolific "writer" of the spirit world was a girl who reportedly died in the seventeenth century but returned as a spirit control in the early years of the twentieth century. The spirit called herself Patience Worth.

Patience operated through the agency of Mrs. Pearl Curren, a St. Louis housewife who was interested in spiritualism. On July 8, 1913, while Mrs. Curren was using a Ouija board, this message came through:

"Many months ago I lived: Again I come—Patience Worth my name." Later Patience provided details of her life. She was born in England in the seventeenth century, migrated to America, and was killed by Indians. But she failed to provide the sort of information that could be checked historically. In other respects, however, Patience was very chatty.

She progressed from the Ouija board to speaking directly through Mrs. Curren while Mr. Curren took down the dictation. She even learned to operate a typewriter using Mrs. Curren's fingers.

Patience turned out an incredible stream of stories, poems, sermons, and aphorisms which some people thought had literary merit.

A St. Louis newspaperman named Caspar W. Yost wrote articles and finally a best-selling book on the subject. Patience's own writings were also extremely popular. There were Patience Worth clubs and even a magazine devoted to her.

But interest faded, and the writings of Patience Worth which enchanted so many in the early years of the twentieth century, seem almost unreadable today.

# HARRY HOUDINI

Harry Houdini was probably the greatest, and he was certainly the most famous, magician of modern times. Houdini is best-known for his dramatic escapes from straightjackets, jail cells, sealed coffins, and the like. But late in his career he was also well-known for his fierce opposition to spirit mediums.

Some believe that Houdini became interested in spirit mediums after the death of his mother. He had always been very close to his mother, and it was thought that he was desperately anxious to contact her "beyond the grave" if possible. But as he went to one medium after another he found that they were fakes, and this enraged him. A more prosaic explanation is that Houdini saw that the mediums were using the same sort of tricks that he and other magicians used on stage, but were claiming that they possessed real supernatural powers. Exposing them was good publicity.

Whatever Houdini's motives he did carry out a number of highly publicized exposures of popular mediums.

*Harry Houdini awaiting another great escape. (UPI/Bettmann)*

He soon came to be regarded as the medium's foremost enemy.

Houdini died in 1926 as the result of a tragic accident. Houdini told some college students that he had such highly-developed muscular control that he could be hit in the stomach and not feel the blow. One of the students hit him before he had a chance to tense his muscles. The result was a fatal injury. The unexpected circumstances of his death, coupled with the fact that it took place on Halloween, lent it an air of sinister and supernatural significance.

The rumor spread that Houdini had left a coded message with his wife and onstage assistant Beatrice that he was to try and communicate through a medium after his death.

Immediately lots of mediums claimed that they were in contact with Houdini, but Beatrice would not endorse any of their claims for about two years. Then she got a letter from an American medium named Arthur Ford. What followed was an extremely confusing and controversial chain of events.

At first Beatrice Houdini appeared to endorse the genuineness of the Ford message. She even held a séance with him. Then a newspaper reporter said that he had heard the magician's wife and the medium plotting a hoax in order to make money. Some of Houdini's professional colleagues insisted that there had been no message, and that the code, far from being a secret, was a simple one that Houdini and his wife had used when they did a mentalist act on stage. Moreover, the key to the code had been published a few years before the magician's death.

Beatrice Houdini was a troubled woman who had nearly been shattered by her husband's death. She backed away from her endorsement of Ford and said that there never had been a message. However, she denied ever conspiring with the medium, insisting that her illness and fragile emotional state had caused her to become confused. But for several years she did hold séances on Halloween. Finally she gave them up, declaring that if Houdini had survived death, he wasn't coming back.

To this day spirit mediums continue to hold séances on Halloween, and invariably some of them insist that they are in contact with the great magicians spirit. A Halloween ceremony by professional magicians at Houdini's grave attracts so many onlookers that it has caused friction between the magicians and the officials of the Westchester, New York, cemetery where Houdini is buried.

# WALTER THE GUIDE

During the early years of the twentieth century, American spiritualism was dominated by the medium Mina Crandon, known in spiritualist circles as Margery. Margery was the wife of a respectable and prominent professor of surgery at Harvard Medical School. Margery's spirit control was her dead brother Walter, who had been killed in a train accident in 1911.

Margery became well-known outside of spiritualist circles in 1922 when she tried to claim a prize offered by the magazine *Scientific American* to anyone who could show genuine mediumship. One of the members of the magazine's committee who was to judge the genuineness of the phenomena produced by the medium was the magician Harry Houdini, already known as a fierce opponent of mediums and spiritualism.

Margery, with Walter's aid, had apparently produced some astonishing effects in several séances where Houdini was not present, and by 1924 it seemed as though the prize was hers. But Houdini objected, and more séances were arranged in which the magician imposed strict controls. He designed a cabinet in which the medium could be enclosed, leaving only her head and hands visible.

During one of the séances a folding ruler was found in the cabinet. Houdini accused Margery of smuggling the ruler into the cabinet so that she could manipulate a small box containing a bell that was supposedly rung by spirit hands. Walter, on the other hand, accused Houdini of planting incriminating evidence, and during the séances he became very abusive and threatening. In the end the committee decided not to award Margery the prize. However, after Houdini's death in 1926 one of his assistants admitted that he had placed the ruler in the cabinet on Houdini's instructions. Naturally spiritualists jumped all over this confession. Surprisingly some magicians also think Houdini may have framed the medium because he hated her and knew that she was a fraud, but had been unable to prove it.

Later there was other, and more definite proof of Margery's trickery. One of the most compelling pieces of evidence that Margery offered for Walter's existence was that during a séance he would impress his thumbprint in a piece of dental wax. However, an investigator found that Walter's thumbprint was identical to that of Margery's dentist. The dentist apparently had nothing to do with the fraud, and of course Margery never admitted or explained anything. Despite the fingerprint fiasco and other exposures, Margery dominated American spiritualism for many years.

# ROSALIE

On December 15, 1937, Harry Price, who was England's most famous ghost hunter, went to a séance in "one of the better-class London suburbs." Later when he wrote the event up he went to great lengths to disguise the identity of those involved.

He called his hosts Mr. and Mrs. X. A friend of the family was a Frenchwoman Price called Mme. Z. She had been married to an English officer who had been killed during World War I, leaving her with an infant daughter. The tragedy for Mme. Z was compounded when the girl, Rosalie, died in 1921.

Beginning in 1929, Mr. and Mrs. X began holding regular séances with Mme. Z at which the spirit of Rosalie almost always appeared.

Harry Price was an experienced psychic researcher and well aware of the fact that many séances were faked. He had exposed many of these fakes himself, and he went to great lengths to make sure that this one was above suspicion.

After Price took elaborate precautions, the séance began. There were six participants, Mr. and Mrs. X

HARRY PRICE LIBRARY, UNIVERSITY OF LONDON

*This drawing shows the arrangement for the Harry Price séance in which he spoke with "Rosalie."*

and their daughter, Mme. Z, Price, and a young man he called Jim. After a few minutes in the dark Mrs. X whispered to Price that Rosalie was in the room. He heard the shuffling of feet, and when he reached out he touched what he took to be a little girl of about six years of age. He was even able to feel her pulse.

Price had brought some luminous plaques which cast a dim greenish light. He was allowed to uncover the plaques, and in the faint light he saw what he described as "a beautiful child who would have graced any nursery in the land."

The séance ended a short time later though it was two years before Price published a report of the event. When it was published it created a sensation. In the report he said that he was convinced that the séance could not have been faked.

There was an immediate clamor for more information. Price insisted that he would have to respect the privacy of those who were involved. Later he said that at the end of August 1939 the X family and Mme. Z went on a motoring tour of France but the war broke out, they were separated, and Mme. Z disappeared, presumably taking the spirit of Rosalie with her.

Price resolutely refused to provide any additional information. All efforts to find out more about Mr. and Mrs. X, Mme. Z, even the house in which the séance presumably was held have come to nothing. Surely "Jim" or someone who had attended an earlier séance at which the spirit appeared, or some of the servants or neighbors should have come up with some supporting evidence for the story. But no one ever did. It all depended on Harry Price's word. By that time Price had become involved in other investigations; he simply stopped talking about the little girl ghost. He seemed to regret that he had ever written about Rosalie in the first place, but he never admitted that he had not told the truth.

# THE GHOST HUNTER'S GHOST

Harry Price was England's best-known ghost hunter for nearly forty years. He was a prolific writer, and his sometimes controversial investigations were always extensively reported in the press.

Price died in March, 1948, and a few months later there was a report that he came back—as a ghost.

At about the time Price died a young Swedish man, who is known only as Erson, awoke to find an elderly, slightly balding man standing by his bedside. The figure began to speak to Erson in a language that he did not understand but that he took to be English. The figure was able to get across to Erson the information that his name was Price.

The figure that called itself Price appeared regularly, not only to Erson, but to his wife and daughter. Since he was confronted by an English-speaking apparition, the young Swede tried to learn a little English and was able to hold at least a rudimentary conversation with his ghostly visitor.

Price told Erson that he had been involved in the investigation of ghosts. He also urged the young man to go to a particular hospital for the treatment of a difficult health problem. At the hospital Erson met a doctor who was also interested in psychic research. He was able to identify the ghostly figure as Harry Price, a man Erson had never heard of. Why the spirit of the ghost hunter should appear to a man in another country who did not know him and had no interest in his work and did not even speak his language was something no one could fathom.

# ELVIS

Surveys indicate that around eight percent of the American public does not believe that Elvis Presley is dead. They think that for some obscure reason the King of Rock 'N' Roll faked his own death, and that he is now living under an assumed name and identity somewhere in the U.S. Elvis "sightings" have become as familiar a part of the American scene as UFO sightings.

Yet the evidence that Elvis did indeed die on August 16, 1977, at his Graceland mansion in Memphis, Tennessee, is overwhelming and utterly convincing.

So if people have really been seeing Elvis since August 16, 1977, they have either been fooled by the ever-growing army of Elvis impersonators or they are seeing a ghost.

Here is a typical case. On December 20, 1980, a truck driver named Jack Matthews was hauling a load to Memphis. About a hundred miles outside of Memphis he picked up a hitchhiker. He was a young man with a Tennessee accent who said that he was going to Memphis to see his "momma and daddy" for the holidays. It was dark, and the hitchhiker was wearing a big hat, so Matthews could not see him clearly. But he was pleasant and polite, and they talked mostly about cars, a subject that fascinated both the driver and his passenger. The hitchhiker mentioned that he owned several Cadillacs. Matthews figured he was just boasting.

As the truck rolled into the outskirts of Memphis there were more lights, and Matthews was able to get his first good look at the hitchhiker. He looked familiar. And when the hitchhiker said he wanted to be dropped off on Elvis Presley Boulevard, he knew why. The fellow looked like Elvis.

The ride was almost over when Matthews realized that he had never introduced himself. "My name is Jack Matthews," he said.

The hitchhiker looked straight at him and said, "I'm Elvis Presley, sir."

Matthews said something like "You've got to be kidding." But he knew his passenger wasn't kidding, and the more he looked at the man, the more he realized that he *was* Elvis Presley.

An elderly Tennessee farmer named Claude Buchanon, who had known Elvis slightly, said that the singer's ghost appeared to him shortly after his death, and before the news of his death was broadcast on the radio or television. All the figure said was, "I've come to say good-bye for a while, Claude."

Over the years there have been hundreds, perhaps thousands, of similar accounts.

# II.

# Haunted Places

# A PREHISTORIC GHOST

Perhaps the oldest ghost recorded anywhere in the world is that of a prehistoric man who gallops on horseback along a road in the English county of Dorset.

The first written account of the ghost came in a letter from a Mr. R. C. C. Clay, an antiquarian, who was doing excavations in the area. In 1924 he was driving home at dusk one evening, when he saw a horseman ride out of a clump of trees near the road. As he drew closer:

"I could see that he was no ordinary horseman, for he had bare legs, and wore a long, loose cloak. His horse had a long mane and tail, but I could see neither bridle nor stirrup. His face as turned towards me, but I could not see his features. He seemed to be threatening me with some implement, which he waved in his right hand above his head.

"I now realized that he was a prehistoric man, and I did my best to identify the weapon so that I could date him. After traveling along side my car for about a hundred yards, the rider and horse suddenly vanished. I noted the spot, and found next day, when I drove along the road in daylight that it coincided with a low, round barrow [a prehistoric grave site] which I had never noticed before."

Though Clay kept looking for the horseman, he never saw the figure again. But others did. When he asked a local craftsman about the ghost, the man replied matter-of-factly, "Do you mean the man on the horse that comes out of an opening in the pinewood?"

About two years later he got a letter from an archeologist friend:

"Your horseman has turned up again. Two girls, cycling from Handley to a dance at Cranborne (the area where he had seen the ghost), have complained to the police that a strange looking man on a horse had followed them and frightened them."

There are many prehistoric burials in the area, and men of the Bronze Age, probably chieftains, were sometimes buried with their horses. So this appears to be not only the ghost of a prehistoric man, but of a prehistoric horse as well.

# HAUNTED BATTLEFIELDS

There are many accounts of ghostly armies refighting their battles. Reports of phantom armies come from every land and every age. The earliest ones that we know of come from the Assyrians thousands of years ago.

According to legends, ghosts have been seen at the battlefield in Marathon, where in 490 B.C., the ancient Greeks dealt a crushing blow to the invading Persians. It was said that anyone who visited the battlefield after sunset heard the clash of the swords, and the screams of the wounded and dying, and that they smelled the odor of blood. Anyone who actually saw the ghostly warriors was reportedly dead within a year. It was not a place that people liked to visit at night.

One of the best-known of all haunted battlefields is located just seven miles outside of the English town of Banbury. It is a place called Edgehill. On October 23, 1642, the first major battle of the English Civil War between the supporters and opponents of King Charles I was fought at Edgehill. Four thousand were said to have died in the battle, which neither side really won.

On Christmas Eve of that year, shortly after midnight, a group of shepherds and travelers in the vicinity of the battlefield saw the whole engagement fought all over again by two ghostly armies in the sky.

The king was so impressed by the account that he sent six trusted officers, headed by Colonel Lewis Kirke, to investigate. The six visited the spot themselves. In their report to the king they said that they had seen the ghostly battle with their own eyes. Some members of Kirke's group insisted that they recognized among the ghosts many who had fallen at Edgehill.

After these first reports hardly a year passed without people telling of an appearance by the ghostly armies of Edgehill.

The forces of Charles I were crushed two years later at a place called Marston Moor. From time to time people have reported seeing a full-scale ghostly reenactment of this battle as well.

Another type of haunted battlefield experience was reported by the Lieutenant John Scollay, commander of a group of Scottish Highlanders, fighting in France in the opening days of World War II. The men were pinned down in a wooded area outside of the French town of Dunkirk. Though the Highlanders were normally the bravest of soldiers, they seemed to lose their will to fight. The men told their commander that they had to get out of there, because the wood was haunted.

"It's just a presence, sir," explained one of the soldiers, "but we've all felt it. It's a kind of force pushing us away. And it's something that none of us can fight, sir—something uncanny."

Eventually the Highlanders joined the other British troops in a general retreat. Once out of the "haunted wood" Scollay's men regained their fighting spirit. But they could do nothing about the overwhelming odds. Most were either killed or taken prisoner.

Lieutenant Scollay himself was taken prisoner and spent the rest of the war in a German POW camp. When he was released after the war, Scollay did some research in the library at Dunkirk. He found that in the summer of 1415, a few months before the decisive battle of Agincourt between the English and the French, there had been another battle fought in that "haunted wood."

Scollay wondered if the spirits of those long-dead soldiers had somehow come back to torment their successors some five hundred years later. Or was the area so filled with an aura of death that the Scots were able to sense it?

# THE SAMURAI GHOSTS

On April 24, 1185, a great sea battle was fought in Japan between two powerful samurai clans, the Genji and the Heike. The battle was fought near a place called Dan-no-ura. It ended in an overwhelming defeat for the Heike.

The Heike commander committed suicide, and the grandmother of the boy emperor, a member of the Heike clan, jumped into the sea carrying the child. Practically every one of the Heike samurai drowned himself. So did all the members of the Imperial court.

The sheer scale of the horror left a profound impression on the Japanese. The story was told and retold in many ways throughout the centuries. And for centuries sailors avoided the area of Dan-no-ura. They feared they might catch sight of the restless ghosts of the Heike, who had been condemned to wander the area for eternity.

Peasants reported seeing ghostly armies bailing out the sea with bottomless dippers. It was said that they were attempting to cleanse the sea of blood, a task that could never be accomplished.

The ghosts were supposed to try to sink ships, or pull down anyone foolish enough to swim in such a cursed sea. On the beach ghostly fires that are supposed to be the restless spirits have been seen. The wind is said to have a peculiar sound, like the shouting of thousands of voices or the clamor of battle.

The strangest of all the legends surrounding this terrifying event concerns the crabs that live in the area. They are called Heike crabs. The shell of each crab appears to bear the image of a human face. The crabs are supposed to contain the spirits of the dead samurai.

# THE BLOODY TOWER

Tourists visiting the Tower of London, one of England's foremost tourist attractions, hear a great deal about its bloody history and its ghosts. The Tower was first built over eight hundred years ago, and has been considerably altered over the centuries. It was long used as a prison and place of execution.

No one knows how many people have been executed there, probably thousands. The victims have ranged from common folk to kings and princes. Perhaps the most notorious event in the Tower's history is the imprisonment and probable murder of the two little princes. Twelve-year-old Edward V and his ten-year-old brother were locked up in the Tower in 1483, a time of political turmoil. They were never officially executed, but they were never seen again either, and it is assumed that they were murdered. Suspicion naturally fell on their uncle, the Duke of Gloucester, for with the boys out of the way he could become king. That is exactly what he did, assuming the title Richard III.

For nearly two centuries the Tower was said to have been haunted by the ghosts of the two princes. In 1674 workmen came upon a wooden chest containing the skeletons of two young boys. It was assumed that these were the remains of the princes, and they were given a royal burial. Since that time the boys' ghosts have not troubled the Tower.

Sir Walter Raleigh was imprisoned in the Tower for thirteen years. On moonlight nights his ghost can be seen walking back and forth along the upper walls near the room where he was kept.

In 1605 Guy Fawkes led a plot to blow up the Houses of Parliament. The plot was betrayed and Fawkes was horribly tortured before being executed in the Tower. His screams can still be heard echoing through the Tower corridors.

Of all the Tower Ghosts the most famous by far is Anne Boleyn, the second wife of Henry VIII. When Anne failed to present the king with a son he decided to get rid of her. Instead of divorcing her he had her beheaded in the Tower in 1536.

Of all Henry's wives Anne Boleyn has always been the most popular and her execution did the most to damage Henry's reputation. Anne's ghost, both with and without its head, has been reported frequently in the Tower.

The best-documented sighting came in 1864. A guardsman at the Tower was to be court-martialed for falling asleep while on duty. He defended himself by saying that he encountered the ghost of a woman coming out of the room where Anne spent her last night before execution. He said the sight so terrified him that he fainted. When several other guards stepped forward to say that they, too, had seen the phantom the charges were dismissed.

There are some rather curious apparitions reported at the Tower. Around 1800, a guard near the Jewel Tower, where the Crown Jewels of England are kept, reported seeing a huge black bear standing on its hind legs. He struck at it with his bayonet, but the bayonet passed right through it.

In 1817 Edward Swifte, keeper of the Crown Jewels, encountered what looked like a large cylinder filled with a bubbling blue liquid. He struck out at it with a chair, but the chair went right through it. The form then retreated and disappeared. Years later Swifte recalled, "Even now ... I feel the horror of that moment."

# THE GREEN GHOST OF VAUVERT

In the mid–thirteenth century the very pious King Louis IX of France gave a house near Paris to six monks from the Order of St. Bruno. However, from the window of their new house the monks could see a much finer residence nearby. It was the palace of Vauvert. The palace had been built as a royal residence by King Robert, but had been unused for many years.

Vauvert, though deserted, never had the reputation of being haunted until the monks of St. Bruno became its neighbors. From then on, frightful shrieks and howlings were heard from the palace every night. People reported seeing strange lights in the windows of the deserted palace. Finally a huge green specter with a long white beard was seen regularly at an upstairs window, howling and shrieking at passersby.

The stories of these ghostly goings-on at Vauvert soon reached the ears of the King himself, who was shocked and sent a commission to investigate. The monks of St. Bruno also professed to be shocked, but they hinted to the commission that if they were allowed to inhabit the palace, they would soon expel the ghost.

The king was relieved and delighted to hear that the holy monks offered to undertake the dangerous task of getting rid of the ghost. A deed was drawn up making the palace of Vauvert the property of the monks of St. Bruno, and once they moved in the disturbances ended forever.

Though solid information on this case is scanty, there is good reason to believe that it is an early example of a ghostly fraud.

# THE GHOSTLY MONKS OF GLASTONBURY

There is no more mysterious, legend-enshrouded place in England, or indeed the entire world, than Glastonbury Abbey. Glastonbury may be the site of the oldest Christian Church in the British Isles. But long before it was a Christian church Glastonbury was a pagan place of worship.

Legend has it that Christianity and perhaps the Holy Grail were first brought to Glastonbury by St. Joseph of Arimathea, the wealthy man who was supposed to have taken Jesus' body and placed it in the tomb he had prepared for himself.

King Arthur is said to have been taken off to Glastonbury after his final battle. In fact, the historical King Arthur may really have been buried at Glastonbury, though there is no firm evidence of this. Certainly King Arthur's ghost has been reported there.

One of the most unusual ghostly accounts connected with Glastonbury took place early this century. The antiquary and archaeologist Frederick Bligh Bond and his colleague, J. Allan Bartlett, were appointed to take charge of excavations at the ancient abbey.

Bond and Bartlett were also firm believers in the spirit world. While at the abbey they experimented with automatic writing. One of the men held a pencil in his hand, and the pair talked casually. Sometimes the man holding the pencil would find his hand beginning to write. He was not supposed to guide the pencil himself. His hand was believed to be under the control of some sort of outside intelligence.

The first message came through on the night of November 7, 1907. It contained a drawing of a floor plan of Glastonbury, and it was signed Gulielmus Monachus—William the Monk. Messages from other monks, all of whom indicated that they had lived at Glastonbury in about the thirteenth century, followed.

The ghostly monks began sending messages about the original construction of the abbey. They told the archaeologists what they would find and where to dig. This was information that no mortal could know.

On the basis of these messages the two archaeologists claimed to have unearthed a chapel, the existence of which was previously unknown and unsuspected.

Critics, however, complained that the information produced by the automatic writing contained much that was demonstrably wrong and nothing that could not have been gathered by examining existing historical records or from careful observation and deduction.

At the time the Glastonbury messages were the subject of a lively controversy which has never really been resolved.

# GRIM GLAMIS CASTLE

Glamis Castle is a grimly imposing fortress in Scotland. There are many ghostly and ghastly legends associated with it, the most celebrated being that of the secret room.

In the eighteenth century the castle was the home of the earls of Strathmore. It was said that there was a hidden and locked room in the castle that contained a hideous secret. The secret was known only to the earl himself, his heir, and the steward of the castle. The secret was to be revealed to the heir on his twenty-first birthday.

Usually the heirs to the earldom made light of the idea of a secret until they turned twenty-one, then they changed. They became morose and suspicious. In 1876 one heir saw what the secret had done to his father, and he absolutely refused to be enlightened about it.

His wife, however, was extremely curious about the mystery and she once asked the steward what the secret was. The steward gravely assured her, "If your ladyship did know, you would not be a happy woman."

In 1880 a Scottish newspaper reported that a workman had accidentally stumbled across the secret room. A short time later he disappeared and it was rumored that he had been given a large sum of money and told to emigrate to Australia and never reveal to anyone what he had seen.

There is supposed to be a ghost in the room, but the most popular theory is that the room once contained one of the heirs to the estate. According to this theory in 1821 the first son of the eleventh earl of Strathmore was born horribly deformed and was not expected to live. The family put out the information that he had died shortly after birth, but he was really placed in the secret room for what was expected to be a very short life. However, contrary to medical predictions, the deformed infant did survive.

When a second son was born and became heir to the estate, his deformed eldest brother, the true heir, was still alive and locked in the secret room. This secret had to be imparted to him and to all who wrongfully inherited the earldom. In fact, the deformed heir outlived four earls of Strathmore, and each had to be told of the hidden chamber and what it contained.

It was also said that the earls of Strathmore actually encouraged rumors of ghosts in order to draw attention away from their real secret.

But there are plenty of other ghostly tales at Glamis. There is a gray lady, supposed to be the ghost of Janet Douglas, wife of James, sixth earl of Glamis. She was suspected of poisoning her husband. Later she was tried and executed for witchcraft. Another variation of the legend is that she was walled up in the secret room and her powers of witchcraft have kept her alive there even today.

There is the gruesome tongueless woman who looks out of a barred window, or runs across the park, pointing at her bleeding mouth. There is even a vampire legend at Glamis. This is the tale of a woman servant at the castle who was caught in the act of sucking blood of one of her victims. She was said to be walled up alive (or at least undead) in the secret room which—if all the legends are to be believed—must be pretty crowded. However, that is not the proper way to get rid of a vampire. The danger that someday the wall may be broken down and the evil creature once again released within the castle still exists.

# HAUNTED HAMPTON COURT

Cardinal Wolsey, principal advisor to King Henry VIII, had a magnificent palace called Hampton Court built for himself on the River Thames outside of London. The king coveted Hampton Court, and when the cardinal died he appropriated it, and it soon became one of his favorite residences.

It's haunted, of course, primarily by some of Henry's six wives. The king's third wife, Jane Seymour, bore him a son at Hampton Court and died a week later. Her ghost has been reported gliding along the area known as the Clock Court, carrying a lighted candle.

The most famous and tragic of the Hampton Court ghosts is that of Lady Catherine Howard, another of Henry's wives. Henry had her arrested, and she was ultimately executed at the Tower of London. On the night of her arrest at Hampton Court she broke free from her captors and raced along the gallery in an attempt to see her husband and plead for her life. Henry, who was in the chapel, ignored her pleas, and she was dragged away shrieking and sobbing.

On the anniversary of her arrest her ghost is said to come shrieking down what has come to be known as the Haunted Gallery. Her screams are also reportedly heard in the little room from which she escaped and to which she was dragged back.

The most persistent of the Hampton Court specters is a tall, gaunt woman in a long gray robe. She has been identified as Mrs. Sybil Penn, nurse for Henry's children. She was much loved by those she had cared for and was given a pension and an apartment in Hampton Court. When she died on November 6, 1586, she was buried at nearby St. Mary's Church.

All was quiet for a couple of centuries until Mrs. Penn's grave and monument were moved, and her remains scattered in the process. A short time later the family that occupied her old apartment at Hampton Court began hearing strange noises The most persistent noises were those of a woman's voice and a spinning wheel.

In an attempt to locate the source of the noises a wall was torn down and inside was found a sealed chamber that contained among other things a very old spinning wheel, one that may have belonged to Mrs. Penn.

It was about that time that the gray-robed figure began to be seen in the halls and around the apartment. There is a statue of Mrs. Penn at Hampton Court, and the gray lady is supposed to resemble that figure.

# THE CALVADOS HAUNTING

In 1875 a large country house in France called Calvados Castle was rocked by a series of violent, and well-recorded ghostly disturbances.

The owner of Calvados has shielded his identity under the title Monsieur de X. He lived there with his wife and son, the son's tutor, Abbé Y, and four servants.

Monsieur de X described the events in great detail in his journal. The abbé's room seemed to be particularly afflicted. There were loud bangings on the wall. A heavy candlestick moved across the mantelpiece by itself. An armchair that had been securely fastened to the floor inched its way toward the fireplace.

At the end of October, M. de X wrote: "A very disturbed night. It sounded as if someone went up the stairs with superhuman speed from the ground floor, stamping his feet. Arriving on the landing he gave five heavy blows, so strong that the objects suspended on the walls rattled in their places. Then it seemed as if a heavy anvil or a big log had been thrown on the wall, so as to shake the house." No source for the sounds could be discovered, and there was worse to come.

In mid-November, a new type of noise was added. "... everybody heard a long shriek, and then another, as if of a woman outside calling for help. At 1:40 [A.M.] we suddenly heard three or four cries in the hall, and then on the staircase."

Over the following days the shrieks became more alarming. "It is no longer the cry of a weeping woman, but shrill, furious despairing cries, the cries of demons or the damned."

Windows and doors opened and closed by themselves. Furniture was thrown around. The invisible thing, whatever it was, then began to attack people. Mme. de X was struck in the hand with such force that the mark was visible for days.

Finally a priest was called in who performed the rites of exorcism and placed religious medals throughout the house. Here M. de X's account ends, but we can not be entirely sure that the exorcism ended the strange manifestations.

# THE HOBY GHOSTS

The fate of poor little William Hoby has been used to frighten generations of students. William was the son of Sir Thomas Hoby, who lived in England in the sixteenth century during the reign of Henry VII.

Both of little William's parents were brilliant and energetic, though his mother had always been considered a bit odd. Aside from being a scholar learned in several languages, Lady Hoby has also been described as being "a pest of outstanding quality."

Poor William inherited none of his family's intellectual gifts. Not only was he a slow learner, he was sloppy as well. During his lessons he would become so nervous that he always left inkblots on his copybook. Lady Hoby was severely disappointed in her son's abilities, and the sight of a blotted copybook absolutely enraged her. William was frequently beaten because of his poor schoolwork. One day, when presented with another blotted copybook, Lady Hoby became so enraged that she completely lost control of herself and beat the boy to death.

The place where William died is called Bisham Abbey. It was said to be haunted, not only by the ghost of the unfortunate William, but by the ghost of Lady Hoby as well. The ghost of Lady Hoby has been seen washing her hands in a basin which floated in front of her. She was trying to wash off the bloodstains. One unusual feature of this particular ghost sighting is that the specter of Lady Hoby was often seen "in negative"—that is, with a black face and wearing a white dress.

In the nineteenth century renovations were made to Bisham Abbey. Behind one of the walls was found a number of badly blotted copybooks. According to tradition these were the very books which drove Lady Hoby to her murderous fury.

After World War II the abbey was taken over by a sports organization and converted into a gymnasium and hostel for students. The Hoby ghosts have not been reported since that time.

# THE WEIR HOUSE

During the seventeenth century Major Thomas Weir was regarded as one of Edinburgh, Scotland's most upstanding citizens. To the outside world he seemed a man of undisputed honesty and fierce, almost-fanatical religious piety. He was the last person in Edinburgh anyone would have suspected of engaging in evil practices. So one can imagine the shock when, in the year 1670, Major Weir, who was then about seventy years old, suddenly confessed to a long series of crimes, including witchcraft.

At first it was assumed that Major Thomas had gone mad, and the assumption was probably correct. But Major Weir was extremely persistent in confessing his crimes, and some doctors examined him and declared him to be sane. So he was finally brought to trial, convicted, and executed along with his sister, who was implicated in the crimes.

The case of Major Weir became quite famous, but it arose at a time in history when the witchcraft hysteria was beginning to die down in Scotland. That is probably why the major had so much trouble getting people to take his confession seriously at first. Yet the Weir case remained famous long after people stopped believing in witchcraft. The gloomy Weir house on the street called the Bow in Edinburgh became the center for what was now regarded as all manner of ghostly rather than diabolical activities.

People reported seeing a spectral coach drive to the door of the house in order to take the major and his sister to hell. No one would live in the place, and it remained vacant for a century. Finally one old couple was induced to move in because of the low rent. The next morning they fled, swearing that a calf had gazed at them through a window while they were in bed. Just why this should have terrified them so is not recorded. The house remained empty and falling down until 1830, when it was finally demolished. During the entire period, the Weir house may well have been the most famous haunted house in the whole world.

A book called *Traditions of Edinburgh,* published in 1825, states, "His [Major Weir's] house, though known to be deserted by everything human was sometimes observed at midnight to be full of lights and heard to emit strange sounds as if of dancing, howling, and what is strangest of all, spinning. Some people occasionally saw the major issue forth from the low close [alley] at midnight mounted on a black horse without a head, and gallop in a whirlwind of flame."

Just before the house was torn down, the novelist Sir Walter Scott testified to the hold it retained on the popular imagination:

"Bold was the urchin from the high school who dared approach the gloomy ruin at the risk of seeing the Major's enchanted staff parading through the old apartments, or hearing the hum of the necromancer's wheel, which procured for his sister such a character as a spinner."

# THE BROWN LADY

Many of the stately homes of England are reputed to have a ghost of one sort or another wandering the corridors. But the ghost of a lady in a brown dress that haunts Raynham Hall in Norfolk is the most famous of them all.

There is a story that in 1786 the Prince Regent, later to become King George IV, was sent screaming into the corridor in his nightshirt when the Brown Lady walked into the guest bedroom in which he was sleeping. The Prince Regent left in the middle of the night and swore that he would never stay at Raynham Hall again—and he didn't.

During the Christmas season of 1835 a certain Colonel Loftus was a guest at Raynham Hall. He got a good look at the ghost. He described her as being a noble-looking woman wearing a brown satin dress. Her face was bathed in an unearthly light. But what was truly frightening was that she had no eyes! Where her eyes should have been there were only empty sockets.

Colonel Loftus made a sketch of what he saw and a painting was made from the sketch. The painting was then hung in the room where the ghost was seen most frequently.

A few years later the novelist Frederick Marryat decided to challenge the ghost. He asked to sleep in "the

*The mysterious figure on the staircase at Raynam Hall, which has come to be known as the Brown Lady. (Photo: Shira)*

haunted room" where the painting hung. One evening Marryat and two companions saw a strange figure carrying a lamp gliding along an upstairs corridor. They hid behind a door. Light from the lamp reflected off the figure's brown dress, and as she passed the door she turned her eyeless face toward them and grinned in a "diabolical manner."

Marryat was carrying a pistol and he fired point-blank at the figure. If someone had been trying to play a joke the hoaxer would have been shot dead. But the bullet passed right through the figure, which promptly disappeared.

The most celebrated appearance of this ghost came in 1936, when two photographers from the magazine *Country Life* were taking pictures of the interior of Raynham Hall. They were photographing the main staircase of the house when a shadowy figure of what appeared to be a woman in a veil came down the stairs. They took a picture and when it was developed it showed a dim and ghostly-looking figure on the stairs. The film has been examined by photographic experts who do not believe that it is a fake.

This picture of the Brown Lady of Raynham Hall is considered to be one of the best and most mysterious of the many photographs that people claim to have taken of ghosts.

# THE COCK LANE GHOST

The modern era of ghost hunting began in the mid-eighteenth century with strange happenings in a house on a little London street called Cock Lane.

The house was owned by a man named Parsons. The ghost was that of a Miss Fanny, a distant relative of a stockbroker named Kent who rented the Cock Lane property from Parsons. Miss Fanny had come to serve as Kent's housekeeper after his wife died.

Kent and Parsons quarreled about money. Kent moved out and sued his former landlord. At about this time Miss Fanny died, apparently from smallpox. Parsons hinted darkly that Miss Fanny had been poisoned by his enemy Kent.

In 1762, about two years after the death of Miss Fanny, stories began to spread that the Parsons's house in Cock Lane was being haunted by the ghost of poor dead Fanny. Elizabeth Parsons, daughter of the owner, a girl of about twelve, said that she had seen the ghost and the ghost said that she had been poisoned. No one else actually reported seeing Miss Fanny, but many claimed that they heard the knocking and scratching noises the ghost made.

According to Elizabeth the ghost would not make itself visible but would answer questions by using a simple knocking code, one knock for yes, two knocks for no. A loud scratching sound indicated extreme displeasure.

A committee was appointed to investigate the case. They questioned the ghost and were told that she had been poisoned and that Kent would be hanged for the crime. Further tests were held, some quite dramatic, and the case was a sensation throughout London.

However, there were skeptics. It was found that when Elizabeth was not present, or that when someone held her hands, there were no knocks in response to questions.

Kent now took the offensive. He sued Parsons, his wife, a servant in the house, and a printer whom they had hired to publish an account of the haunting. The trial was held on July 10, 1762, and the judge found all the defendants guilty and gave them stiff sentences. Parsons and his associates never admitted guilt, and some people continued to believe that the ghost was real.

Many years later a man named J.W. Archer visited the crypt in which Miss Fanny's body had been entombed. He opened the coffin and found that the body inside had been remarkably well preserved. It showed no signs of smallpox, the disease which was supposed to have killed the woman. He also recalled that some poisons help to preserve a body.

This was an eerie footnote to the case.

# THE HYDESVILLE HAUNTING

The large and influential movement that came to be known as spiritualism began with a rather common series of events in upstate New York. In March 1848 the small cabin of farmer John D. Fox in Hydesville, New York, was shaken by an outbreak of strange noises of unexplained origin. The house was occupied by Fox, his wife, their two young sons, and his two youngest daughters Margaret or Maggie and Kate (also called Katie, Cathie, or Catherine), who was not quite twelve. The noises came from the room in which Maggie and Kate slept. So far this seemed like a fairly typical poltergeist case.

The next step was to attempt to communicate with whatever it was that was making the noises. One night, when the girls were in a rather playful mood, they began asking the unknown noisemaker some questions. To everyone's surprise they began getting answers to the questions. When they asked the age of one of the girls, the correct number of knocks was given. This so astonished Mr. and Mrs. Fox that they called in some of the neighbors.

Such "rapping poltergeists" had been heard in the past, but not in the Hydesville vicinity. As word of the spirit rappings spread, hundreds flocked to the Fox house to witness the marvel.

The rapping spirit indicated that in life he had been a traveling peddler who was murdered and his body buried in the cellar of the house by its previous occupant. The Foxes dug up the cellar, and according to one account they found some human teeth and bones and parts of a broken bowl. But this story, like so much about the case, has been disputed.

The Foxes worked out a rapping code that could be used to send messages more complex than yes or no. The first message delivered in this code was "We are all your dear friends and relatives."

Suddenly the phenomenon had been expanded dramatically. Instead of being simply messages from a murdered peddler who may have been seeking revenge, a channel of communication to the world beyond the grave seemed to have been opened. Just four years before, Samuel Morse had made his first successful experiments with the telegraph. Now it seemed a "spiritual telegraph" had been discovered.

Under the guidance of their older sister Leah and a local hypnotist, Dr. George Capron, the girls began giving public performances, which were enormously popular. By 1850 they were drawing huge crowds in New York City.

There were plenty of skeptics who thought the whole thing was a fake. But there were many influential believers as well. Even confessions of fraud by relatives and former associates of the Fox sisters couldn't shake their faith. The success of the Fox sisters stimulated many others to become mediums, some of whom became more famous and successful than the Fox sisters themselves. The spiritualist movement that they had started had outgrown them and passed them by.

In 1888 the large spiritualist community was rocked when Maggie and Kate Fox made public statements that they had faked the Hydesville rappings from the beginning and that spiritualism itself was a fraud. They said the whole thing had begun as a childish joke to frighten their parents, but they were swept up in the excitement and the money they made.

By this time both sisters had lost whatever money they had obtained over the years. They were paupers and alcoholics. Convinced spiritualists refused to believe their confessions and said that they became turncoats for money.

Ultimately Maggie recanted her confession and was accepted back into the spiritualist fold.

# THE OCTAGON

The Octagon is one of Washington, D.C.'s most historical houses. It is also one of its most haunted houses.

The Octagon was built in the early 1800s for John Tayloe, a Virginia plantation owner. Shortly after the building was finished Tayloe was supposed to have had a serious quarrel with one of his eight daughters. The girl grabbed a candle and rushed up the huge oval staircase. There was a scream and her body plunged down the stairwell to the ground. Whether she fell over the railing or jumped is a matter of controversy.

The daughter's restless spirit is said still to haunt the stairway. Some nights a flickering candle is seen going up the stairs. When it reaches the top there is a shriek, followed a second later by a sickening thud.

The death of his daughter greatly affected Tayloe. Some said that he was haunted by her spirit. Whatever the reason, he stayed away from his Washington mansion most of the time.

During the War of 1812 the British entered Washington and burned many of the buildings, including the White House. Tayloe contacted President James Madison and offered the Octagon as a temporary home while the White House was being rebuilt. Madison accepted the offer and moved into the Octagon in the fall of 1814.

The President's wife Dolley Madison was a well-known party giver, and she held elaborate receptions at the Octagon. Years after the Madison era, newspapers carried accounts of apparitions of footmen in full uniform of that period hailing cabs. They quoted some who said they had heard the sounds of wheels rumbling over gravel roads, the opening and closing of carriage doors, and the fading sounds of carriages rolling away.

Some visitors to the house have reported seeing the ghostly form of Dolley Madison herself standing in front of the mantelpiece in the ballroom, where she customarily received her guests. The spirit was easy to recognize, for it wore a tall turban headdress. Dolley Madison was acutely conscious of being very short, and she often wore a big turban to make herself look taller.

After the Madisons moved out the Tayloe family moved back in, and there was another tragedy, grimly similar to the first. Another of the Tayloe daughters had eloped against her father's wishes. She returned home to beg his forgiveness. The two met on the staircase. The angry Tayloe tried to brush past his daughter. The girl either lost her balance or fell trying to get out of his way. She tumbled down the stairs and broke her neck. The spot at the foot of the stairs at which her body came to rest is always supposed to be abnormally cold.

According to legend there are other spirits at the Octagon as well, including that of a young girl who was killed by her jealous lover and whose body was sealed inside of a hollow wall.

The Octagon's haunted reputation was so great that a lot of people wouldn't live there, and the old place deteriorated greatly. It wasn't until the 1960s that attempts were made to save and restore this historic old house. But even today there are occasional reports of ghostly happenings, everything from the scent of a strange perfume suddenly filling a room, to a photograph of what some people say is the ghost of Dolley Madison slipping into the house through a rear door.

# THE CHELTENHAM HAUNTING

One of the famous and closely investigated cases of a haunting in England involved a large Victorian house at Cheltenham in the county of Gloucestershire. The house was called Garden Reach.

The house was built in the 1860s and purchased by a man named Henry Swinhoe. He lived there for some years with his wife. When she died he became a changed man and began drinking heavily. After about two years he married a woman named Imogen, who thought she could reform him. She failed and quickly turned to drink herself.

The couple quarreled violently. Mostly they quarreled about the first Mrs. Swinhoe's jewels, which Henry had hidden somewhere in the house. He wanted them to serve as a nest egg for the children of his first marriage. Imogen thought she should have then. Imogen left her husband before his death in July 1876. She died a few years later but left instructions that she was to be buried in a churchyard in Cheltenham, just two miles from the house in which she had lived so unhappily.

Garden Reach was empty for some years until in April 1882, when it was rented by a Captain F.W. Despard. The haunting began a few months later. The principal witness in this case was the family's eldest daughter Rosina, who kept a detailed record of the events. At the time she was in her twenties, a highly intelligent and strong-willed young woman. She went on to become a doctor—very unusual for a woman in Victorian times—and held several important medical posts. Rosina Despard was a first-rate witness.

One evening in June she saw "the figure of a tall lady, dressed in black standing at the head of the stairs. After a few minutes she descended the stairs and I followed for a short distance, feeling curious what it could be. I had only a small piece of candle and it suddenly burnt itself out, and being unable to see more, I went back to my room."

This was just the first of many encounters that Miss Despard and others had with the strange figure. She was described as "... a tall lady dressed in black of a soft woolen material, judging from the slight sound in moving. The face was hidden by a handkerchief held in the right hand ... As she held [her hand] down, a portion of the widow's cuff was visible on both wrists, so that the whole impression was of that of a lady in widow's weeds."

It was always assumed that the ghost was that of Imogen Swinhoe, still looking for those hidden jewels.

Dogs were sensitive to the ghost's presence, cats failed to react at all. Once a group of children tried to make a ring around the ghost, but it eluded them.

When the haunting began the ghost had a very substantial shape, but as time went on it became less distinct. After 1886 it had assumed a very ghostly appearance indeed. It seemed to disappear entirely after 1889, though soft footsteps were reported until 1892.

After about ten years the Despards moved out of Garden Reach. The house was turned into a girl's school. Reports differ as to whether the ghost was ever seen there. According to one account there was so much trouble with the ghost that the proprietors finally abandoned the school.

There have also been reports of the ghost being seen in some neighboring houses.

# THE *GREAT EASTERN*

She was to be the largest and fastest steamship ever built. And she was going to revolutionize and dominate sea traffic between England and Australia. That was the dream of Isambard Kingdom Brunel, a successful builder of bridges and railroads. And Brunel was able to sell his dream to a large number of investors. But the dream quickly turned into a nightmare.

The great ship was built in London's best shipyard. Its most revolutionary feature was to be its double hull, two iron skins three feet apart. The ship named the *Great Eastern* was literally a ship within a ship, with a sealed compartment separating the two. The outer skin could be torn, but the great ship would remain afloat.

During the last stages of the construction one of the workmen, a master shipwright, disappeared. He had been working on the double hull, and a rumor spread that he had been accidentally sealed inside it.

Launching was scheduled for November 2, 1857. Shortly before the scheduled launch a strange hammering sound was heard inside the *Great Eastern*. No one knew where it came from and it was soon forgotten in the excitement of the moment.

However, as the launching began the great ship got stuck. And the mysterious hammering sound started again. The builders decided to wait until the next high tide for the launching. That didn't help.

Over the next few weeks further attempts were made to launch her. They were all frustrated for one reason or another. By the end of November people began to wonder if the *Great Eastern* would ever be launched. The more superstitious sailors began to say that the ship was jinxed or haunted.

It wasn't until March of the following year that spring tides and heavy rains finally eased the ship into the river. By that time the delay had cost so much that Brunel's company had gone bankrupt. Brunel himself died during the summer of 1859, a few weeks before his ship actually steamed into the open sea. On the day of his death hammering was again heard aboard the *Great Eastern*.

Once at sea, one of the smokestacks exploded, killing six crew members and doing extensive damage to the ship. It took months before she was repaired. However, once the ship began her London to Australia run her first three trips went without mishap, and it looked as if the jinx was broken. But on the fourth trip there was a huge wave which nearly capsized the ship. She was so badly damaged that she drifted through the night, and the crew, thinking that they were about to die, broke into the storeroom where the liquor was kept. Guns were issued to passengers so they could protect themselves from drunken sailors.

Everyone survived, but the great ship's days as an ocean liner were finished. She was stripped and set to the mundane task of laying cable in the North Atlantic. When that task was finished, in 1866 she was put up for sale. There were no bidders.

The once-mighty *Great Eastern* was a derelict for nearly twenty years until she was sold for scrap. As the ship was being towed on her last journey, the lone watchman aboard began hearing the thud of hammer blows. He could not locate the source of the noise. Then the lines hauling the wreck broke, and she was nearly grounded on the coast.

When she was finally brought to the scrapyard and cut apart workmen made a gruesome discovery. In the space between the double hull was a skeleton. Next to the skeleton was a carpetbag of rusted tools. It was the remains of the master shipwright who had been entombed during the final stages of construction.

# GRIEF

In Washington, D.C.'s old Rock Creek Cemetery is a large bronze statue by the celebrated sculptor Augustus Saint-Gaudens. The statue of a shrouded, lonely-looking figure bears no inscription. It is commonly called *Grief* because it is said to inspire feelings of sadness in those who see it.

The monument was commissioned by the historian Henry Adams to mark the grave of his wife Marian.

Adams was a member of one of America's most prominent families. The great-grandson of President John Adams, the grandson of President John Quincy Adams, he was a distinguished scholar in his own right. Marian also came from a prominent family and was regarded as a well-educated woman, fully the intellectual equal of her husband. In the late 1870s Adams left his teaching position at Harvard and settled in Washington. Marian's health began to decline and she became a virtual invalid, though no one seemed to know what was wrong with her.

Then one cold winter evening Adams returned home to find his wife unconscious before the fire. She never recovered and died a few days later. Adams said virtually nothing about his wife's death, and tried, with considerable success, to keep all of the circumstances surrounding the death quiet. Inevitably rumors multiplied.

The most persistent was that a deeply depressed Marian Adams committed suicide.

When Adams commissioned the monument he told the sculptor that "no . . . attempt is to be made to make it intelligible to the average mind." Rock Creek Cemetery officials didn't think the memorial a proper one and resisted having it placed in the cemetery, but the influential Adams prevailed.

Later Henry Adams was to write his autobiography, considered one of the great American autobiographies. But he never once mentioned his wife.

Stories of Marian Adams's ghost began to circulate just a few years after her death. People were said to have seen the ghost sitting in a rocking chair in the bedroom of the house in which she died. Then there would be a loud scream, and the ghost would vanish.

The house is no longer there, but the stories have been transferred to the monument. One groundskeeper recalled how the statue seemed to come to life, and that the eyes appeared to stare out from the shadows of the cowl that nearly covers the forehead and sides of the face.

Another story is that people who have visited the monument at dusk are sometimes joined by the form of a woman dressed in the clothing of the late 1880s.

If it had been Henry Adams's intention to obliterate his wife's memory, he did not succeed.

# THE ABANDONED LIGHTHOUSE

There is only one known case of the keepers of a lighthouse abandoning their post. The place was the Eilean Mor Lighthouse on an island off the west coast of Scotland. This was an exceptionally remote and stormy spot, even for a lighthouse, and for that reason the lighthouse was an important one.

On the night of December 15, 1900, the brigantine *Fairwind* was sailing near the Eilean Mor Lighthouse. Sailors saw a lifeboat cut directly across the bow, heading for the lighthouse. But the men in the lifeboat looked pale and ghostly. The sailors first thought they had come upon a boatload of corpses from some shipwreck. But they could see the arms of the rowers moving. The lifeboat soon disappeared from view.

Later that night a storm broke. It was then that passing ships noticed that the Eilean Mor light was out. Fortunately there were no wrecks caused by the absence of the light, but there were plenty of worried and angry skippers.

At first they thought that something was temporarily wrong with the light. But days passed, and it did not go on again. There were three men who tended this light. If one of them had become ill or even died, the others surely would have been able to restart the light, or send some sort of distress signal. There was nothing.

It wasn't until the day after Christmas that a supply ship went to the lighthouse to investigate. The lighthouse was empty, and the searchers could find no reason why it should be deserted. The searchers found two oddities. The men's foul-weather gear, oilskins and seaboots, was gone. They also found shreds of seaweed, of a variety unknown in that region.

But the strangest revelation was yet to come. In the logbook kept by Thomas Marshall, the head lighthouse keeper, there was a description of a terrible storm that lashed the lighthouse for three days starting December 12. "Never seen such a storm," he wrote. The log indicated that the men were badly frightened and spent the time praying and crying. The final entry in the book, December 15, one day after the light went out read only "Storm ended, sea calm. God is over all."

There was no hint as to what actually happened to the three men. What puzzled everyone was that there had been no storm on the days indicated by Marshall in his log. In fact, on the island of Lewis, a mere twenty miles away, the weather had been unusually calm. A storm began on the night of the fifteenth.

An official inquiry into what had happened could reach no conclusion. But residents of nearby islands had their own explanation. They had always believed the islands were haunted, and only fools, like those who kept the lighthouse, dared to stay on them overnight.

The local people believed that the ghosts of shipwrecked sailors sometimes came ashore to claim the living.

# THE BERKELEY SQUARE HORROR

For many years the house numbered 50 in London's fashionable Berkeley Square was regarded as one of the most fearfully haunted houses in all England. But just exactly what it was supposed to be haunted by was never known.

Reports of a haunting first began in the 1850s. There were strange noises, objects were thrown about, windows were even broken. In addition several people who lived in the house said that when they touched the walls they "are found saturated with electric horror." The ghost is often called The Electric Horror.

By the 1890s the Horror had become associated with a single room in the house. The house had also begun to attract a lot of attention. Lord Lyttleton, member of a family that had more than its share of supernatural experiences, demanded that he be allowed to spend a night in the room. He armed himself with two blunderbusses loaded with buckshot and silver coins. These took the place of silver bullets.

The next morning he said that something had come into the room and jumped through the air at him, but he was able to fire one of his blunderbusses at it, and it disappeared. When asked to describe what it was that had entered the room he could not.

Sir Robert Warboys was not so lucky. He was a

deeply skeptical man and boasted to his friends that he could spend a night in the haunted room. It was arranged. Several of his friends were to stay downstairs in the house. Sir Robert was armed with a pistol, and there was a bell he could ring if he needed help.

Sometime after midnight, as his friends were dozing in the drawing room, they heard a violent ringing of the bell from upstairs. They rushed up to the room which Sir Robert had occupied and found him sprawled half on the bed with his head near the floor. The pistol lay on the floor. It had not been fired.

He was dead. His eyes were open and staring, and his lips were drawn tightly back over his teeth. As far as anyone was able to determine he died of fright.

After that story got around it became impossible to rent 50 Berkeley Square for any price, and the house remained vacant, until just before Christmas of 1887, when two sailors from the frigate *Penelope* who had squandered all of their money started looking for a place to sleep. They came upon the empty house in Berkeley Square. It was beginning to snow, and they decided to spend the night inside rather than risk freezing.

The sailors knew nothing of the history of the house and found the second floor bedroom the most inviting place to stay.

At around two in the morning a policeman walking his beat near Berkeley Square was accosted by an hysterical and nearly incoherent sailor. The man told a confused story about how he and a companion broke into an empty house and were assaulted by something—he couldn't describe what it was. Somehow he managed to escape from the house. But he was terribly afraid for his friend.

The sailor practically dragged the policeman to No. 50. The front door was open. There at the bottom of the stairs was the body of the second seaman. He had been trying to escape from the house, but he hadn't made it. There was an indescribable look of terror in the dead man's eyes which was to trouble the policeman in his dreams for the rest of his life.

The house never was rented and finally was torn down.

# THE WINCHESTER MYSTERY HOUSE

One of the strangest houses in America is a monument to a wealthy woman's obsession with ghosts.

Sara Winchester was the widow of William Winchester and heir to the great Winchester firearms fortune. Winchester died in 1880, and the couple's only child died the same year. This double tragedy left Sara Winchester in a deep depression from which she could not be shaken.

Like many in the late nineteenth century Sara Winchester turned to spiritualism for solace. A spirit medium who claimed to be in touch with her dead husband told Sara that she was to build a house for the spirits of all those who had been killed by Winchester rifles.

The widow sold her home in Connecticut and headed West, believing that her husband's spirit would guide her to the proper destination. When she got to the Santa Clara Valley in California she saw a large house under

*The Winchester Mystery House shown in an aerial view where all its sprawl and turrets can be seen. (Courtesy the Winchester Mystery House)*

construction. She felt that the spirit told her that this was the place and she immediately arranged to buy the uncompleted house from its owner, a California doctor.

She wanted some changes in the building plan, but as she described them to the builder he thought they were insane and quit the job. Sara Winchester didn't have to worry. For the kind of money she was willing to pay she could find plenty of willing workers who would follow even the maddest of plans.

For the remaining thirty-six years of Sara Winchester's life, she devoted much of her time and fortune to building, tearing down, and otherwise altering her "ghost house." Though she was constantly changing her mind she was always in a hurry; the building went on seven days a week. Sara believed she was getting her plans directly from the spirit world and the spirits would not wait.

The final result was what has been described as the largest private home in the world. It can also be described as a mad jumble. There are stairways that lead nowhere. Elevators that go to only one floor. Doors that open onto blank walls or, worse, to sheer drops.

The outside of the house is just as mad as the inside. There are peaks and spires all over the top of the structure. Rooms and entire wings seem to be stuck on randomly. The whole thing was generally hidden from public view by great hedges and high trees that kept a crew of gardeners constantly at work.

The construction of the house had a sort of mad logic behind it. Dictated by a fear of evil or vengeful spirits, Sara Winchester may have been trying to confuse them in the maze of corridors and dead ends. It was said that she would sleep in a different bedroom every night, and when she slept in every bedroom in the house, she would begin the rotation all over again. Ghostlike herself, she often wandered the corridors at night.

There was a small windowless chamber called the Blue Room. Her Sara held regular séances. Sara was also said to hold regular banquets. The table was always set for thirteen, but Sara herself was the only visible diner.

Sara Winchester died in her ghost house in September 1922 at the age of 85. The house is now run as a tourist attraction, and is a very popular one.

# THE HAUNTED U-BOAT

The U-boat, underwater boat, or submarine was one of the most effective weapons used by the Germans during World War I. As the war dragged on the Germans rushed the construction of more U-boats at the shipyard at Bruges, in occupied Belgium.

One of these boats, known only by its number U-65, seemed jinxed from the start. Several workers were killed during its construction. On the day it was launched one of its officers was swept overboard and drowned. The first underwater test was nearly catastrophic. U-65 was unable to surface for nearly twelve hours. No reason for the malfunction was ever discovered.

A day after the malfunction there was a more serious accident. A torpedo exploded on deck and a second lieutenant and five crewmen were killed. Most of the later stories of haunting center around the second lieutenant. Tales began to circulate that the ghost of the dead lieutenant had been seen on the ship. "We saw him come aboard and walk slowly to the bow. He stood there, staring at us, with his arms folded across his chest," said one crewman.

The stories began to affect the morale of the entire crew seriously. One man who claimed to have seen the ghost deserted and was never seen again.

After several comparatively uneventful months at sea

U-65 docked at Bruges for routine maintenance. While the captain and crew were ashore there was an Allied attack on the city and the captain was killed in the bombardment.

The German High Command needed this ship, and denounced rumors of a jinx and haunting as "superstitious nonsense." The admiral who headed the U-boat command actually spent a night on U–65 and said that he had seen no ghosts. But just to be on the safe side he had a minister come in to exorcise the ship.

The new captain was a tough disciplinarian. He said that anyone who reported seeing a ghost would be severely punished. It didn't work. One of the crew's most trusted members rushed into the control room screaming, "I've seen the ghost—an officer standing near the bow torpedo tubes." The man was so hysterical that he had to be locked up. After he calmed down he was released, but as soon as he had a chance he grabbed a bayonet and stabbed himself to death.

The demoralized crew now tried to avoid all possibility of dangerous contact with the enemy, but the ship was still struck by shellfire and had to limp back to Bruges for repairs. The head of U-boat command was furious. He had the captain and crew replaced.

U–65 came to a mysterious end. On the morning of July 10, 1918, an American submarine spotted U–65 lying on the surface off the southern coast of Ireland. The ship seemed deserted, and the Americans decided to blow it up, but as the Americans were preparing a torpedo U–65 was torn apart by a violent explosion.

Just before she blew up, the American captain said he thought he saw someone standing on the ship near the bow. The figure appeared to be that of a German officer wearing a navy overcoat. It stood there unmoving, with its arms folded.

# BORLEY RECTORY

There are many places which have been given the title of "England's most Haunted House." In the 1930s most would have handed the title to an ugly red brick structure called Borley Rectory.

Borley Rectory was built in 1863 by Rev. H.D.E. Bull. Like many old houses in England, Borley had its ghosts; a spectral nun who was supposed to walk the grounds was the ghost most commonly reported. The Reverend Bull died in 1892 in the Blue Room of the rectory. He was succeeded by his son the Reverend Harry Bull. The second Reverend Bull also reported seeing the ghost, and he said the ghost did unusual things like throw mothballs around. But Rev. Harry Bull was a man with a lively sense of humor, and it is quite impossible to know when he was making a joke.

This Reverend Bull died in 1927, also in the Blue Room, which came to be known as the Haunted Room. At the time of his death mothballs were said to have been found all over the room.

The third set of tenants were the Reverend and Mrs. Eric Smith. They did not have the easy tolerance of the supernatural that the Bull family seemed to possess. It was reported that one of the ghosts they saw was that of the second Reverend Bull. There were also doorbells that rang mysteriously, pebbles that were thrown at windows, and other poltergeist-like activity. All of this came to the attention of Harry Price, England's premier ghost hunter.

Price went down to Borley in 1929 and witnessed some of the poltergeist phenomena. The next year the Smiths moved out and Rev. L.A. Foyster (a relative of the Bulls) and his wife, Marianne, moved into the rectory and stayed for five years. It was during this period that the unusual activities seemed to reach their peak. Most centered around Marianne, who was a troubled woman, much younger than her husband. She claimed that one night she had nearly been smothered by the ghost. Price and other ghost hunters came back, and were impressed by what they saw. Borley Rectory was getting quite a reputation.

The Foysters left in 1935 and the new clergyman refused to live in the place. Harry Price then had an opportunity that he had sought for years, the chance to live and work in a real haunted house. He leased the property for a year and brought in a team of volunteer researchers. The results were published in the book *The Most Haunted House in England*. The book was extremely popular and first hailed as a milestone of psychic research.

But Price had his detractors, even among psychic researchers. They began to chip away at his evidence. After Price's death in 1948 there were a series of revelations, including reports that Price had been caught faking evidence. Mrs. Smith, wife of one of the former residents, said that Borley Rectory had never been haunted by anything worse than rats, and that the stories about what she and her husband were supposed to have seen were untrue.

A careful investigation of Price's original notes, as compared to what he wrote in his book, indicated that at the very least Price exaggerated what he had actually seen and heard. In fact, very little out of the ordinary happened while Harry Price was at Borley.

Price had his defenders, but the revelations left his reputation severely damaged. Borley Rectory itself had burned to the ground in 1939, taking its secrets, if it ever had any, with it.

Even today, though Borley no longer exists, visitors still come to the area hoping to catch a glimpse of the spectral nun, or otherwise get in touch with the supernatural.

# DEADLY CROSSINGS

Railroad crossings have often been the scene of terrible accidents. Sometimes a ghost, or ghostly impression of what took place appears to linger.

In 1978 an English couple driving through the countryside had to pass over a rail line at a spot called Utterby Halt. There were no gates or signals at the crossing so the driver approached very cautiously. But as soon as the car moved onto the tracks it stopped dead for no apparent reason. The driver was unable to restart the engine, and the couple began to fear that a train might come along and hit them.

They decided that they should get out of the car and off the track. But before they were able to do this the car was buffeted by a violent gust of wind, which shook the vehicle. Then there was a loud roaring sound like that of an oncoming train. The combination of wind and sound so terrified the couple that they were virtually paralyzed. They were sure that a train was heading right for them.

The whole incident lasted less than a minute. It was followed by an eerie silence, and then quite suddenly the driver was able to restart the car. They drove a short way and looked back. The track was rusty and choked with weeds. The line had obviously been abandoned for some time. They could find nothing to account for their strange experience.

Later they discovered that in 1953, before the line was abandoned, a railway worker had accidentally stepped out in front of a fast-moving freight train at Utterby Halt during a dense fog and had been killed instantly. In the 1920s a woman had been killed in a similar accident at the same spot, and there had been several other serious, but nonfatal accidents at the crossing.

Here is another example of a deadly crossing. On March 1, 1948, a group of German prisoners of war in England were riding in a truck which was struck by a train at a place called Conington. Six of the prisoners were killed and five more seriously injured. Once again the reason for the accident appears to have been dense fog.

About a year later, Col. A.H. Mellows and his favorite dog, a Labrador retriever, were killed while driving across the same spot. Colonel Mellows was buried with full military honors. His dog was buried near the spot where the accident took place.

Since that time there have been many strange experiences reported at the crossing. The crossing gate would often be found swinging open mysteriously, after it had been securely locked. Several railroad workers reported seeing a large black car, of the type Colonel Mellows was driving, pull up to the crossing, and then simply disappear. Those who did not actually see the car said they heard the crunch of gravel, as an invisible car approached the tracks. Years later, long after the old crossing had been changed and completely modernized, local people continued to regard it with fear.

# ROADSIDE PHANTOMS

There are many accounts of a ghost appearing at the spot where a violent death took place. For that reason it is not surprising that many ghosts are reported at or near the site of a fatal auto accident.

But the tradition of roadside phantoms predates the automobile age. On a quiet road between Marlborough and Hungerford in England is a small stone cross inscribed with these words: "A.P. Watts, May 12, 1879." It is a memorial to a fourteen-year-old boy, Alfie Watts, who had been killed when he was struck by a heavy horse-drawn cart at that spot. Villagers erected the small stone monument to his memory.

Over the years memories fade, and the cross itself was often hidden by grass and wildflowers. In October 1956, Frederick Moss and three friends were driving home from the movies at night when the headlights of the car suddenly picked up a tall, thin, clean-shaven man standing right in the middle of the road. He wore a long brown coat and stood with his back to the spot were the cross was hidden in the grass.

Moss hit the horn and the brakes. The man didn't react. Moss had the awful feeling that he might have run over the fellow. With his companions he searched the area, but they found nothing.

Moss told the story to his wife. She had been born in the area, though it was long after the accident that killed Alfie Watts. She did, however, remember the boy's father, Henry Pounds Watts, who died in 1907. The figure her husband described sounded like the Henry Watts she remembered seeing when she was a very young girl.

Why had this ghost suddenly chosen to appear after all those years? There was a plan to widen the road, and if that happened the little cross might be destroyed. The father may have wanted to remind people that the modest memorial should be preserved when the road construction took place.

If that was the ghost's mission, it certainly succeeded, for when the road was widened the little cross was carefully replaced nearby.

More commonly, however, it is the ghost of the victim himself, or herself, that is encountered. In America there are hundreds of accounts from drivers who are suddenly confronted by a figure in the road. They try to stop, but can't. When they get out to try to find the person they believe they have just hit, they find nothing. Later they are told that the person they describe actually was hit by a car and killed years earlier at that very spot.

One person said that after believing that he hit someone, he actually found what appeared to be body on the road. He went for the police, but when they returned, there was nobody to be seen. He discovered that the incident took place at the site of an earlier fatal accident.

# III.

# Animal Phantoms

# PHANTOM DOGS

"'Footprints.'

'A man's or a woman's?'

Dr. Mortimer looked strangely at us for an instant, and his voice sank almost to a whisper as he answered:

'Mr. Holmes, they were the footprints of a gigantic hound!'"

That is a passage from "The Hound of the Baskervilles," the best-known of all Sherlock Holmes stories. It concerns the legend of a gigantic and supernatural dog that appears to bring doom on generations of the Baskerville family.

Arthur Conan Doyle, creator of Sherlock Holmes, got his idea for the story when he heard tales of a phantom or spectral hound that was supposed to roam the bleak landscape of Dartmoor, bringing destruction to all who had the misfortune to see it. Appropriately Doyle set his story in Dartmoor.

There are similar tales told all over England, indeed all over the world. These phantoms are known by many different names. In the part of England called East Anglia the dog is called Black Shuck. He pads silently beside lonely roads ready to jump out on unwary travelers. He is about the size of a small calf, and his enormous yellow eyes glow in the dark. It is said that anyone who meets the creature is destined to die within a year.

In Lancashire a similar creature is called the Trash hound and in Yorkshire it is Padfoot. In the north of England it is Striker, and in many other places it is simply the Black Dog.

In the town of Tring in Hertfordshire, there is a tradition that a phantom dog appears from time to time at a place where a woman was hanged for witchcraft hundreds of years ago. Here is an early nineteenth century description of this animal:

"I then saw an immense black dog just in front of our house. It was the strangest-looking creature I ever saw. He was as big as a Newfoundland dog, but very thin and shaggy. He had long ears, a long tail, and eyes like balls of fire. When he opened his mouth we could see long teeth. He seemed to grin at us. In a few minutes the dog disappeared, seeming to vanish like a shadow or sink into the earth."

Though the tradition of the phantom dog is no longer as strong as it once was, even today there are those who still believe that such an animal appears as an omen of death.

# THE WHITE RABBIT OF CRANK

In seventeenth century England belief in witchcraft was still powerful. In the tiny village of Crank in the county of Lancashire, there was an old woman who was suspected of being a witch. She was a foreigner and lived in a little cottage with her granddaughter Jenny. The old woman made a small living by concocting herbal remedies. Though the only potions she was known to have sold were medicines, there were rumors that she also made poisons.

Among her customers was a man named Pullen, a violent and miserly man, who had contracted a serious disease. He went to the old woman and paid what he considered an enormous amount of money for a potion, but it didn't help. In fact, he got worse, and Pullen became convinced that the old woman had not only cheated him but poisoned him.

In order to break what he considered a spell she put on him, Pullen determined to kill the woman. He enlisted the aid of an evil character named Dick Piers. The pair put on disguises one night and crept to the old woman's cottage. They attacked her and she cried out, waking Jenny, who was sleeping in the next room. The girl was badly frightened and grabbed her beloved pet white rabbit. Clutching the rabbit, she went into her grandmother's room and saw the two men. They saw her as well.

Still holding the rabbit, the girl ran from the house, with Pullen and Piers in hot pursuit. She disappeared over the crest of a hill, and when the pair got to the top all they could find was the rabbit. Swearing, Piers killed the animal with a single kick.

The men now abandoned the plan to murder the old woman, but they were still responsible for a death. When Jenny ran from the cottage in terror, she fell into a ditch, hit her head, and died.

Everyone in the village suspected Pullen and Piers, but nothing could be proved. The old woman had not seen her attackers clearly, and she was generally thought to be a witch and a foreigner to boot. However vile Pullen and Piers might be, they were local men.

That might have been the end of it. But one night as Piers was walking home across the fields he saw a white rabbit, and was convinced it was the ghost of the white rabbit he had killed. This terrified him, and memory of the crime began to weigh on his mind. Finally he confessed what he had done to some friends. The next morning he was found at the bottom of a local quarry. He had either jumped or fallen in, perhaps while running away from something.

Pullen's health continued to decline. One day while passing the old woman's cottage he looked down and saw a large white rabbit hopping along beside him. He ran, but the rabbit ran easily alongside him. The desperate Pullen was able to get just a few yards from his own home when he collapsed with exhaustion and fright. He lingered for about a week, raving about a white rabbit before he finally died.

Even today people in the area say that "the White Rabbit of Crank" can be seen on dark nights. It is considered very bad luck even to catch a glimpse of this creature.

# THE GHOST STEER

Cowboys around Brewster County, Texas, used to tell stories of a ghostly longhorn steer. The animal was branded with the word MURDER. Terrible things were supposed to happen to anyone who even caught a glimpse of the creature.

The story began in 1890. Two brothers, Zack and Gill Taylor, had a dispute over the ownership of a magnificent longhorn steer. The men were quick-tempered and armed, and Zack shot and killed his younger brother.

Almost immediately he was overcome with remorse. When one of the cowhands unthinkingly asked Zack what brand should be put on the steer he replied:

"Put the same brand on him I've got on my hide. Brand him MURDER and turn him loose. I hope he haunts this mesa for a thousand years."

A short time later Zack Taylor shot himself with the same gun he had used to shoot his brother.

Within a few months there were reports of a ghostly longhorn with the brand MURDER on its side. According to the stories the sightings always sparked violence.

A cowboy saw the ghostly animal. When he told two of his friends about it they didn't believe him and called him a liar. He became so enraged that he shot both of them.

A rancher was said to have killed his brother-in-law

in a family argument just a few hours after he had sighted the steer.

A runaway boy who had determined to become a gunman saw the steer on a lonely trail. It frightened him so badly that he decided to turn himself in to the sheriff in the nearest town. When he tried to hand over his guns to the sheriff the gesture was misinterpreted and the sheriff shot the boy dead.

One of the final sightings of the ghost steer came in 1920. A rancher named Faye Dow coveted land owned by Lon Allen and Cole Farrell. He hatched a plot to turn the partners against one another. He convinced Allen that Farrell was trying to steal his girl. He then told the hot-tempered Allen that the best thing to do would be to ambush Farrell.

One night Allen crouched behind some rocks near the trail he knew Farrell would be using. He heard hoofbeats, but what he saw coming down the moonlit trail was not Farrell but a large longhorn steer bearing the brand of MURDER.

The panicky Allen fired four shots into the creature's skull. It didn't even blink. It just looked at him sadly and trotted off into the darkness.

Dow heard the shots and assumed Allen had killed his partner. He rushed to the scene of the shooting, and found Lon Allen in a state of shock. But Allen quickly recovered and figured out what had happened. He then turned his gun on Dow and killed him.

In a very strange trial Allen defended not only himself, but the ghostly longhorn. He said that Farrell had indeed been riding down the trail, and if the phantom had not appeared, he would have been killed.

The jury took only ten minutes to acquit Allen.

# THE DEMON CAT OF WASHINGTON

Underneath the Capitol building in Washington, D.C., is a maze of corridors where it is easy to become lost. These are the haunts of the creature called the Demon Cat.

During the nineteenth century cats were kept at the Capitol to control the population of mice and rats. Eventually other methods of rodent control were used, and the cat population of the Capitol dwindled to nothing—except for the one cat that no one wanted to meet.

Here is how one member of the Capitol guard staff described an encounter with D.C., as the creature is commonly called. The guard was walking down a chilly dark hallway when he saw a shadowy cat walking silently toward him. As it walked toward him it seemed to grow.

The guard felt paralyzed as he stared into the glowing, piercing eyes that came closer and closer and grew larger and larger. The animal grew almost to the size of a tiger. Its purring changed to a ferocious snarl. There was a deafening roar as the monstrous animal leaped—with claws extended—toward its victim. The guard was too terrified to move. He just covered his eyes and waited. But nothing happened. The Demon Cat had disappeared.

Down through the years there have been varied reactions from those who have encountered the phantom. Some have fainted. Some have run screaming from the building. Others, like the guard, became paralyzed with fear. Once an appearance of D.C. may have triggered an elderly guard's fatal heart attack.

The Demon Cat is regarded by some as an omen that always appears just before a national tragedy or on the eve of the changing of the administration.

# THE WEREWOLF'S GHOST

During the early years of the twentieth century Elliott O'Donnell was one of the foremost collectors of British ghost lore. One of the most unusual stories that he recorded was about a ghost who wasn't really human.

The story was told to him by a Miss St. Denis. She had been staying at an isolated farm in Merlonethshire. On many days she would walk several miles to the small railway station to do some sketching and painting. The station was usually deserted.

One day she had stayed later than usual. As she prepared to leave she saw the figure of what she took to be a man sitting on a baggage truck several yards away. She could not see the figure clearly, though it did have what she called "unpleasantly bright eyes," and she knew it wasn't the station master. Suddenly Miss St. Denis became aware of how isolated and gloomy the spot was, and it was beginning to get dark.

She called out, "Can you tell me what time it is?" The figure did not reply, it just continued to stare at her. She packed up her things and began the walk back to the farm, trying to look as jaunty and unconcerned as possible. But as she turned to look back she saw that the figure was following her, and it was getting closer.

It was nearly pitch-dark and she was coming to the worst part of the road. She could scream herself hoarse without the slightest possibility of being heard.

In a sudden burst of courage she turned around and shouted, "What do you want? How dare you!" In the fading light she got her first good look at the thing. It was not human. O'Donnell described it as, "a nude grey thing, not unlike a man in body, but with a wolf's head."

It was ready to spring forward. Instinctively Miss St. Denis reached into her pocket and pulled out a small flashlight. When she shined the light in the creature's face the effect was immediate. It shrank back, and, putting two pawlike hands in front of its eyes, it simply disappeared.

Later Miss St. Denis heard that in one of the nearby quarries some strange bones, partly human and partly animal, had once been found. The few local residents shunned the area after dark, though no one would say exactly why. Wrote O'Donnell, "Miss St. Denis thought as I did, that what she had seen might very well have been the earth-bound spirit of a werewolf."

# THE BIRD OF LINCOLN'S INN

In London there is a large group of buildings located near the law courts called Lincoln's Inn. The buildings are mostly used as lawyers' offices, but one hundred years ago a few rooms were rented out as private apartments. Around 1901 a strange series of events took place which resulted in one of the oddest ghost investigations in history.

One of the apartments had a bad reputation. People who rented it never stayed long. No one could or would say exactly what was wrong with the rooms, but the story came to the attention of Ralph D. Blumenfeld, editor of the *Daily Mail* newspaper.

Blumenfeld asked his friend Max Pemberton, another editor, to help him conduct an investigation by spending one full night in the apartment. The two men went to the third floor apartment just before midnight on Saturday, May 11, 1901. All of the other rooms in the building were offices, so on Saturday night the place was completely deserted.

The apartment was empty except for two chairs and a table in the largest room. This room had two doors, each leading to a small side room. The two investigators searched the place thoroughly, to make sure no one was hidden in the rooms.

Then they spread powdered chalk on the floors of the

two smaller rooms. "This was to trace anybody or anything that might come or go," wrote Blumenfeld.

These preparations completed they sat down at the table in the larger room and waited. They didn't have to wait long. A short time later the doors of the two small rooms began opening and closing by themselves. They examined the small rooms, but there were no marks in the sprinkled chalk. There was no obvious reason for the movement of the doors.

There was a pause and the doors began opening and closing again. After this was repeated several times the men noticed marks in the chalk. But they were not the sort of marks they had expected.

Blumenfeld reported, "The marks were clearly defined bird's footprints in the middle of the floor, three in the left-hand room and five in the right-hand room. The marks were identical and exactly 2¾ inches in size."

Blumenfeld estimated that they were footprints of a bird about the size of a turkey. "There were three toes and a short spur behind ... each one was clearly defined, with no blurring of outline or drag of any sort."

Nothing else happened that night. Blumenfeld's report concluded: "I understand nothing. I am not convinced nor converted nor contentious. I have simply recorded the facts. And the curious thing about it is that my curiosity has not been cured."

For over a century now researchers have puzzled over this strange account of the invisible bird at Lincoln's Inn. Some tend to dismiss it as a hoax, or a newspaperman's practical joke. Others have called it "one of the major mysteries of the ghost-hunters' world."

# TERHUNE'S GHOST DOG

Albert Payson Terhune was America's foremost writer of dog stories in the early years of the twentieth century. In addition to writing about dogs, Terhune also owned a lot of them. One of his favorites was Rex, a large fawn-colored, short-haired dog of mixed ancestry. Rex's appearance was unmistakable. He had a large scar on his face.

Often when the Terhune family sat down to dinner Rex would come to the window and stare in. The dog also spent a lot of time in the hallway sprawled out next to the author's study.

Rex was killed in 1916. A short time later an old friend of the Terhunes, the Reverend Appleton Grannis came to stay with the family. The Reverend Grannis had not seen the Terhunes in many years, he had never seen Rex, and knew nothing about him.

The author and the Reverend Grannis were sitting in the dining room when Grannis suddenly said that he saw a strange dog looking in at the window. Terhune turned, but the dog had disappeared. Grannis said that the animal at the window did not look like any of the dogs he had seen on the Terhune farm, and he described it. The description matched Rex perfectly, down to the scar on his face.

Two years after Rex's death, another friend of the

author's family, Henry A. Healy, insisted that he had seen the figure of Rex lying at his feet when he visited the Terhune farm.

Terhune himself noticed that for years after Rex's death another one of his dogs refused to walk over a spot that had been favored by the dead dog.

# IV.

# Poltergeists

# THE DRUMMER OF TEDWORTH

The first ghost story that was ever really investigated is the case that came to be called The Drummer of Tedworth. It should properly be called a poltergeist case.

The events took place in the town of Tedworth, England, in March 1622. A traveling showman named William Drury was arrested for using counterfeit documents. The local magistrate, John Mompesson, set Drury free but confiscated his drum. Drury had been a drummer in the army and considered the drum an important part of his act. He was very attached to it and very upset when it was taken away from him. Within a few days all manner of strange things began happening in the Mompesson house.

The house was assailed by a loud drumming sound which seemed to grow worse after Drury's confiscated drum was destroyed. The Mompesson children appeared to be lifted out of bed by an unseen hand. Objects were thrown about. In general life became difficult, uncomfortable, and—most of all—noisy in the Mompesson home.

All of this is very typical poltergeist activity, but there was more. One servant was terrified by the vision of "a Great Body with two red and glaring eyes."

The people of the time attributed such phenomena to witchcraft, and the case attracted the attention of Joseph

Glanvill, the chaplain to King Charles II. Though he was a firm believer in witchcraft, Glanvill wanted to establish the facts and not simply be swept along by hysteria and superstition. He went to Tedworth to observe the case himself.

He questioned witnesses, and even heard a few of the strange noises. His book on the subject provides us with the first complete account of the investigations of a poltergeist.

Glanvill concluded that the angry drummer had somehow bewitched the magistrate's house. Early in 1623 Drury was again arrested in a nearby town; the charge was not witchcraft but pig stealing. He was found guilty and sentenced to be transported to the American colonies, but Drury escaped from the convict ship and made his way to a town just a few miles from Tedworth. He bought another drum and began beating it in the town square. Within twenty-four hours Magistrate Mompesson had him arrested on the charge of witchcraft.

Drury apparently confessed or, more accurately, boasted of causing the disturbances, though he would not explain how. Still he was acquitted of the charge of witchcraft, but on the original charge of pig stealing he was again condemned to transportation to the colonies, and this time he did not escape.

Glanvill was told that all the noises and other problems in the Mompesson house had been created by "two young women in the house with a design to scare thence Mr. Mompesson's mother." But Glanvill rejected trickery and blamed witchcraft.

# THE EPWORTH POLTERGEIST

While there have been hundreds and hundreds of poltergeist cases recorded and investigated, the disturbances that took place in the parsonage at Epworth, England, in December and January 1716–17 are among the best-known. The reason so much attention has been focused on this case is that the parsonage at Epworth was the birthplace of John Wesley, founder of Methodism and one of the most influential religious leaders of the eighteenth century.

John Wesley himself was not a direct witness to the strange phenomena, but many members of his large family were. Wesley retained an interest in the events throughout his life, and he always seemed to believe that some spiritual or diabolical force was involved in them.

Toward the end of 1716, the house was afflicted by a variety of strange and inexplicable noises—knocks and rumblings—which reverberated from cellar to attic.

Wrote Mrs. Wesley, "It seemed as if somebody had emptied a bag of money at my feet, and . . . as if all the bottles under the stairs (which were many) had been dashed in a thousand pieces."

When the Reverend Wesley tapped his stick on the floor, the poltergeist would answer with knocks of its own. The poltergeist even disturbed the pious family at its prayers. It became particularly unruly when the names of King George I and the prince were mentioned in a prayer. The Reverend Wesley tried to speak to it but never received any replies. "Only once or twice two or three feeble squeaks, a little louder than the chirping of a bird but not the noise of rats which I have often heard."

Sometimes door latches seemed to rise mysteriously. At other times the Reverend Wesley recalls being pushed against his desk or the wall by an "invisible power." Some strange things were seen, but they were certainly not the traditional ghost. Mrs. Wesley reported seeing something under her bed, "like a badger only without any head that was discernible." One of the hired men saw something that looked like a white rabbit—but not quite.

Most of the disturbances seemed to center around one of the Wesley girls, Hetty, who was about nineteen years old at the time. Not only was she always on the spot when strange noises were heard, she often behaved oddly as well.

After a few months the disturbances simply ended. John Wesley collected written accounts of the events from most of the members of his family who experienced them. Perhaps significantly Hetty never wrote an account of her experiences.

# THE BELL WITCH

Despite the name, the Bell Witch should probably be classed as a poltergeist, though it did a lot of unpoltergeist-like things. Most notably it talked, and once the talking began the "witch" became downright garrulous. It might also be called a haunting or a ghost. It was certainly not a witch. However, back in the early nineteenth century when such a series of events took place they were automatically assumed to be the work of demons or witchcraft in the rural areas of America.

The tale of the Bell Witch began in 1817 on the farm of John Bell in Robertson County, Tennessee. As in many poltergeist cases, the disturbances started slowly. There were the usual strange noises, the rappings and scratchings so typical of poltergeists. Things got worse. Covers were pulled off beds, some of the children were slapped by an invisible hand. The chief target of the witch at this point seemed to be twelve-year-old Betsy, Elizabeth Bell.

At first the family tried to keep the strange events secret. But as the witch grew more active it seemed to affect John Bell's health. The Bells were finally driven to ask for help. Among their neighbors was a lay preacher named James Johnson, who visited the home and declared that there was some sort of evil presence at work. A committee of local residents examined the

*John Bell, a victim of the poltergeist haunting his farm . . . or was it poison?*

facts of the case and decided it was no hoax. The committee called the thing a "witch," and the name stuck.

The witch began to answer questions, first haltingly and in a low whisper. But its voice became louder and more persistent until it could be heard shrieking around the house at any time of the day or night.

The witch gave several different and contradictory accounts of who or what it was. One story was that it was someone who had lived nearby a long time ago and buried a large sum of money. The Bells began digging up their property in search of the treasure. They found nothing, and the witch laughed at them for being so easily taken in.

The witch then announced its intention to destroy "Old Jack Bell." Just why it hated Bell so violently was never made clear. Bell's health continued to suffer. On December 19, 1820, he lapsed into a coma and died. The witch was exultant, claiming it had killed Bell by putting poison into one of his medicine bottles. It was heard shouting and singing at the funeral.

After John Bell's death the witch gradually lost interest in the family. One night several months after the funeral the living room of the Bell house was suddenly filled with smoke. From the midst of the cloud the witch shouted, "I am going and will be back in seven years. Good-bye to all!"

Seven years later the Bell house was again briefly plagued with poltergeist activity.

The story of the Bell Witch became part of Tennessee, and ultimately American, folklore. Many incidents were added to the original account, including an almost certainly imaginary meeting between the witch and General, later President, Andrew Jackson.

Those who have examined records of the case closely suspect that many of the phenomena originated with

Betsy Bell herself. But did she also poison her father? She lived to the age of eighty-three and was very fond of telling Bell Witch stories. She was never prosecuted or even openly accused of being responsible for John Bell's death. Possibly John Bell died from natural causes during the period while the events were going on and local gossip simply assumed that the witch or Betsy was responsible.

# THE FIERY POLTERGEIST

In general poltergeists tend to be annoying but not really dangerous. This was not the case with the poltergeist that manifested itself in the city of Amherst, Nova Scotia, in 1878. It began in the house inhabited by Daniel Tweed, his wife, two young sons, and two of his wife's younger sisters. It was around one of these girls, nineteen-year-old Esther Cox, that the events seemed to center.

First there were strange noises coming from the room in which Esther and her sister slept. Then she woke up with her face and arms horribly swollen. She was in great pain and thought she was dying.

This continued for days. And now there were messages scratched on the wall: "Esther Cox You Are Mine to Kill."

News of these events attracted crowds to the Tweed house, and the strain began to tell on Esther, who was so ill that he could not even get out of bed. She was sent to stay with another sister, and as soon as she was gone the poltergeist activity ceased. But when she came back so did the poltergeist. Now it had a new trick; it began playing with matches, lighting them and dropping them all over the house. There were a number of small fires started, but they were put out before causing serious damage.

Esther said that she could communicate with the spirit. She said that its name was Bob and that it intended to burn the house down, but would not say why. Tweed now suspected that Esther, not a spirit, was the real problem. He ordered her out of the house. She got a job in a local restaurant, but the poltergeist began knocking over chairs and tables. She was fired and Tweed took her back.

A traveling showman tried to capitalize on the poltergeist's fame by putting Esther on stage. It didn't work, because she just sat there and nothing happened, so the audience demanded its money back.

Esther Cox spent the rest of her life wandering from place to place. She served time in prison for arson after being accused of burning down her employer's barn. Esther said the poltergeist did it, but the judge didn't believe her. The unfortunate woman always claimed that the poltergeist had ruined her life.

# V.

# Warnings and Apparitions

# THE SPIRIT OF SAMUEL

The Bible has little to say on the subject of ghosts. The attitude of the ancient Hebrews toward ghosts seems to have been more suspicious than skeptical. Anyone who had dealings with ghosts or spirits of any sort was in some way performing an unnatural and ungodly act, for which he was likely to suffer.

The most celebrated "ghost story" in the Bible recounts just such a case and reveals a great deal about the ancient Hebrew attitude toward ghosts and people who tried to contact them.

Facing a military crisis, King Saul felt that God had turned away from him and denied him access to prophecy. "And when Saul enquired of the Lord the Lord answered him not, neither by dreams ... nor by prophets." So Saul decided to try and obtain his prophecy by other means, by resorting to the practice of necromancy, questioning the dead about the future. Traditionally the dead were supposed to be able to foresee coming events, but to the Hebrews necromancy was an accursed practice.

Still Saul had no trouble finding someone skilled in the accursed art. She was an old woman from Endor, a phrase often translated as Witch of Endor. The King wanted the old woman to summon up the spirit of the prophet Samuel. The woman was very wary because King Saul himself had previously banned all attempts at conversing with the dead and other acts of necromancy on pain of death. But times had changed, and Saul was desperate. He assured the woman that she would not be punished. So she conjured up the spirit of Samuel—"an old man ... covered with a mantle."

The pious old prophet was not at all pleased at having been summoned in so impious a manner. "Why has thou disquieted me to bring me up?" he demanded. King Saul explained that the Lord would no longer answer his questions, but he thought Samuel might. That made Samuel even angrier: "Wherefore then dost thou ask of me seeing the Lord is departed from thee, and is become thine enemy?"

Samuel did issue a prophecy, and it was a grim and terrible one. Not only would the Israelites lose to the Philistines, but Saul and his sons would die in the battle. The next day a completely demoralized King Saul led his army to defeat. His sons were killed in the battle, and in despair Saul killed himself with his own sword.

# THE BLACK VELVET RIBBON

The story of Lady Bersford and the black velvet ribbon that she wore around her wrist has been handed down in the family since the eighteenth century. Though it has been retold in many versions, the account written down by Lady Charles Somerset in about 1857 is the most popular.

Lady Bersford and Lord Tyrone were great friends when they were children. They made a solemn pact that whichever of them should die first, would, if possible, appear to the other.

Even after Lady Bersford was married she continued to see and correspond with Lord Tyrone.

One day she came down to breakfast looking very pale, and she was wearing a black velvet ribbon around her wrist. Her husband asked her if she had hurt her wrist.

She replied that nothing had happened, but continued, "Let me beg you, sir, never ask about this ribbon again. From this day forward you will not see me without it. If it concerned you as a husband, I would tell you at once. I have never denied you any request, but about this ribbon I can say nothing and I beg you never to bring the subject up again."

Her husband was puzzled, but since that was what she so strongly desired he agreed.

Lady Bersford asked the servant if the morning post had arrived. "Do you expect any letters?" her husband said.

"I do," she answered. "I expect to hear that Lord Tyrone is dead, that he died last Tuesday at four o'clock."

A short time later a letter, sealed in black, arrived. She opened it and only glanced at the contents. "It is as I expected," she said. "He is dead."

Her husband looked at the letter. It contained the news of Lord Tyrone's death, which had occurred just exactly as his wife said it had on the previous Tuesday, at four o'clock.

Many years later, when she was dying Lady Bersford

told one of her sons and her closest friend what had happened. She said that she had been awakened by the figure of Lord Tyrone standing by her bedside. He reminded her of the promise they had made when they were children. He then said that he had died last Tuesday at four o'clock.

The specter of Lord Tyrone also made a number of predictions about what would happen to Lady Bersford in the future. He told her that many misfortunes would befall her, but that they were completely unavoidable.

Lady Bersford then said, "When morning comes, I shall believe that all of this was a dream, an invention of my imagination."

"Will not the news of my death convince you?"

"No, I might have had such a dream that had accidentally come true. I will need stronger proof."

The ghost then touched her wrist with a hand that was as cold as marble. In an instant all of the nerves and the muscles were shrunken. "Now," he said, "let no one see your wrist while you live, for to see it would be a sacrilege." The phantom disappeared, and Lady Beresford bound her wrist with the black ribbon, which she never removed.

All of Lord Tyrone's predictions came true, despite the lady's attempts to avoid the worst of them.

When she was dead the ribbon she had worn around her wrist for so many years was removed. Her wrist was exactly as she had described it, with every nerve and muscle shrunk.

# THE RADIANT BOYS

Throughout Europe there are legends of Radiant Boys, the apparition of a young boy, usually surrounded by a glowing light or flame. Some believe that Radiant Boys are just creatures of the spirit world who have taken the form of human boys. However, the majority opinion holds that the Radiant Boys are the ghosts of children murdered by their parents.

Everyone agreed that the appearance of one of these glowing phantoms was a portent of evil to all who saw it.

The most celebrated of the many tales of Radiant Boys is the one about the apparition's appearance to the late eighteenth century English statesman Viscount Castlereagh.

Castlereagh saw the phantom when he was a young man. He was visiting a country house in Ireland and was mistakenly put in what was called ''the boy's room,'' where the phantom was known to appear. He was told by the owner of the house that the boy was the spirit of one of his own ancestors. Many years earlier the boy had been murdered by his mother during a fit of madness. The murder had taken place in the room in which he had been placed.

He was also told that the appearance of the glowing phantom meant two things to the person who saw it;

first he would have a period of great prosperity and power but then at the height of his power he would die violently.

The news did not trouble Castlereagh. At the time he was the second son of a nobleman and not destined to become the heir. His older brother was in excellent health, and he had no reason to expect that his life would be particularly prosperous or powerful. Castlereagh had chosen a military career, and the prospect of violent death was something that every soldier lived with.

But within a short time his life changed completely. His brother was killed in an accident. He became the heir. He also left the army and took up a political career, where he displayed talents that had not previously been suspected. Very quickly he became one of the most powerful men in England.

But Castlereagh was an increasingly unhappy and troubled man. The enormous strains of high office began to take their toll and by 1822 his mental and emotional state began to crumble. He was confined to his country home. His family feared for his safety, so all razors and other sharp objects were removed from his rooms. But on August 12, 1822, Viscount Castlereagh found a pocketknife and used it to cut his own throat.

The prophecy that he had been given many years earlier had come true.

# THE RIVER GHOST

In the early fall of 1777 Rev. James Crawford went out for a ride. Seated behind him on his horse was his sister-in-law Miss Hannah Wilson. When they came to the river, Miss Wilson became frightened. She thought that the water was too high and the current too swift, and that they might be swept away if they tried to cross.

The Reverend Crawford, however, had a different opinion. "I do not think there can be any danger," he said. "I see another horseman crossing just twenty yards in front of us." Miss Crawford also saw the second horseman. The Reverend Crawford called out to the rider to ask if there was any danger.

The rider stopped and turned around, and as he did so the Reverend Crawford and Miss Wilson realized that the rider was no longer human. The face of the rider was ghostly white and fairly glowed with hate and evil. The Reverend Crawford was astonished and terrified at the sight and Miss Wilson was simply terrified. The Reverend turned his horse and rode home as quickly as he could.

He discovered that there was a local belief that the spirit of this ghostly rider appeared in the river every time someone was about to drown. Though the Reverend Crawford had been badly frightened by what he had seen, he felt that it was his duty not to give in to such superstitions. So he declared that he did not believe in warning spirits. However, when he tried to cross the river again on September 27 he was drowned in the attempt.

# LORD LYTTELTON'S DOOM

Lord Lyttelton had a bad reputation, particularly where women were concerned. On the night of November 24, 1779, while he was staying at his London home, he woke up in the middle of the night to find the ghost of a woman standing at the foot of his bed. It was apparently the spirit of a woman that he had wronged, and who had either committed suicide or died of a broken heart. He asked the spirit what she wanted and was told that he had only three days left to live.

On the third day, a Saturday, Lyttelton was with a party of friends at one of his other London houses. He told them of his experience, but said it was only a dream. He insisted that he was in excellent health and that he would surely "bilk the ghost."

Just after eleven, as he was preparing to go to bed with the aid of his servant William Stukey, Lord Lyttelton gave a gasp and collapsed dead in the man's arms.

In another version of the story Lyttelton was more worried about the ghostly prophecy than he let on to most of his acquaintances. He did talk seriously about it to his friend Peter Andrews, and had planned to spend the fatal night at Andrews's house. But for some reason he changed his mind.

At the very moment Lyttelton was dying, Andrews was confronted by the figure of his friend, who cried out, "It's all over with me, Andrews." Andrews first believed that this was a practical joke. But, on the following day, when he heard of Lyttelton's death, he knew it was no joke.

# MARK TWAIN'S VISION

Samuel Clemens, better known as Mark Twain, was about as skeptical an individual as has ever lived. But in 1858, when he was a young man, he had an experience which left him shaken for the rest of his life.

Sam was a cub pilot on the steam riverboat *Pennsylvania,* which ran between St. Louis and New Orleans. His younger brother Henry also worked on the boat, but at a lower position.

While in St. Louis, Sam stayed with his sister and brother-in-law, the Moffetts. One evening shortly before he was due to return to New Orleans Sam had a horrifying dream. He saw his brother's corpse laid out in a metal coffin that had been placed between two chairs in the Moffetts' sitting room. The corpse wore one of Sam's own suits. There was an arrangement of flowers on his chest. All the flowers were white except for a red rose in the center.

*Mark Twain, who was supposed to have received a vision of his brother's death. (UPI/Bettmann)*

The dream had been so vivid that at first Sam had a difficult time convincing himself that it had not been real.

On the trip downriver Sam, who had a quick temper, got into a fight with the master of the ship and was fired. His brother, however, stayed with the ship. Once in New Orleans Sam quickly obtained another pilot's job.

His new ship was running about a day behind the *Pennsylvania,* when he got word that there had been a terrible explosion aboard the *Pennsylvania* just outside of Memphis, and his brother had been severely injured. Sam hurried to his brother's bedside. For a while it appeared as if the young man might recover, but he died suddenly after being given an accidental overdose of painkilling drugs.

When Sam Clemens got to the hospital he found that his brother's body had already been laid out in a metal coffin. Henry was dressed in one of Sam's suits. His own clothes had been destroyed in the explosion. As he watched an old woman came in and put a bouquet of white roses, with a single red rose in the middle on Henry's chest.

Suddenly the dream came back to Sam with painful clarity. All that was missing was the coffin set between two chairs in the Moffett sitting room.

He accompanied his brother's body back to St. Louis. He hurried to the Moffett house. He rushed up to the sitting room. There he found two chairs set six feet apart. The coffin was to be placed on them. That would have fulfilled the final detail of his dream.

# LIEUTENANT SUTTON'S RETURN

On October 2, 1907, James Sutton, a lieutenant at the Naval Academy at Annapolis, Maryland, was shot. According to the official investigation Lieutenant Sutton had been to a dance where he had quite a bit to drink. During a drive back to camp with some of his friends, a fight broke out, and the lieutenant was thrown to the ground. He became enraged and threatened to kill the others. When he got back to camp, he went to his tent and got two pistols. But he was spotted carrying the weapons and told that he was under arrest. Before the authorities could lay their hands on him, Lieutenant Sutton, who was now completely out of control, began to shoot. There was another fight and then suddenly, and deliberately, the lieutenant put a pistol to his head and pulled the trigger.

The lieutenant's family lived all the way across the country in Portland, Oregon. When his mother heard the news that her son was dead by his own hand she could not believe it. She had a vision of her son standing in front of her. "At that instant," she wrote, "Jimmie stood right before me and said, 'Mama, I never killed myself . . . My hands are as free from blood as when I was five years old.'" He said that others had shot him and tried to make the killing look like a suicide.

This vision, or ghost, continued to appear before Mrs.

Sutton for several months. This is not too surprising, considering the tragic nature of the mother's loss. What makes this case interesting and unusual is that the ghost reported several details of the fight and of Lieutenant Sutton's wounds before his mother could possibly have known about them.

In 1909 the Suttons actually had the body, which had been buried in Arlington National Cemetery, exhumed. An examination revealed that many of the wounds that had been described by the apparition but had not been mentioned in the navy doctor's official report did indeed exist.

There were many other troubling details about the navy's handling of the case and there were a large number of unanswered questions. There was no reason given for the initial fight, and there seemed no reason for the lieutenant to have killed himself because of a drunken brawl. The testimonies of the various witnesses were highly inconsistent, an the investigators had refused even to consider the possibility of murder.

No final resolution to this case has ever been reached, and after the exhumation the appearances of the ghost became less frequent until they stopped entirely.

# THE WHITE LADY OF THE OLD PALACE

The Hohenzollerns, once the ruling family of Prussia, were said to be plagued by the specter of a lady in white. She would appear to members of the family shortly before they were to die or suffer a family disaster.

At one point this tale is given a rather curious twist when it is said that the ghost of Frederick the Great, most famous of the Prussian rulers, appeared to his nephew, Frederick William. Frederick William had sent his armies to invade France, but apparently his celebrated uncle did not approve of the invasion.

"Unless you call off the Prussian army from Paris, nephew," said the spirit, "you may expect to see someone who will not be welcome to you."

Frederick William was more frightened by the message than by the ghost itself. "What do you mean?" he asked.

"I mean," said the great Frederick, "the White Lady of the Old Palace. I'm sure you know what happens to those who see her." With that ominous warning the ghost faded.

No one seems sure whose ghost the White Lady of the Old Palace was. Several ladies who had died there in the fifteenth or sixteenth centuries were suspected. How or why she became connected with the Hohenzollerns is also not clear, but she is reputed to have appeared first in 1619 during the reign of John Sigismund. The day after she was seen, John Sigismund died.

Frederick the Great never saw her; as a rationalist and skeptic he didn't even believe in ghosts. According to the legend, however, he changed his mind about ghosts after he became one. The White Lady of the Old Palace was seen in 1806 a few days before Prince Louis of Prussia was killed in a battle with Napoleon's army.

There was also a reported sighting of the White Lady in June of 1914. The ruler at that time was Kaiser Wilhelm II. The kaiser didn't die, but his relative Archduke Francis Ferdinand was assassinated late in June. That was the spark which started World War I. The kaiser survived the war, but Germany was defeated, and the German monarchy was destroyed forever.

# DEATH FORESEEN

Is it possible for a person to see the "ghost" of someone who is not yet dead? Is such an apparition really a ghost? That is a matter of opinion and definition. However, there are many cases in which one individual is reported to have foreseen the death of another. Here is a very striking case that was recorded by the British Society for Psychical Research (SPR).

A man named Jones, who was taking a long walk, got tired and sat down to rest by the side of a river. At first he felt calm and peaceful, but then a feeling of nervousness and even fear gripped him, though he did not know why. He tried to get up but found that he was unable to move. Then what appeared to be a black cloud or fog rose up in front of him. In the middle of the cloud was a man in a brown suit. Suddenly the man in the brown suit jumped into the water and sank out of sight.

Jones was absolutely horrified by his vision. After a few minutes the shock began to wear off and he found himself able to move again. There had been no man in a brown suit—it had all been some sort of hallucination. Nothing had really happened. Still Jones was very upset by what he had experienced, and when he got home he told his sister all about it. She thought it was morbid to dwell on such a subject, and told him to forget it. But he couldn't. The image of the man in the brown suit jumping into the water was too vivid to forget easily.

The next week a man named Espie drowned himself in the river at the very spot where Jones had seen his vision of the man in the brown suit. Espie left a note saying that he had been thinking about killing himself for a long time. However, Jones had never met Espie, and had been completely unaware of his existence. He certainly had no way of knowing what Espie planned to do.

# THE APPEARANCE OF LIEUTENANT McCONNELL

One of the most frequently reported ghostly events is what investigators call "the crisis apparition." The image of a person who has just died, or who is seriously ill and near death, mysteriously appears to a friend or relative who may be tens, hundreds, or even thousands of miles away.

One of the best cases on record took place in England on December 7, 1918, during World War I. Lieutenant David McConnell, a trainee pilot in the RAF, was asked to fly a small plane to a field at Tadcaster, some sixty miles from his home base at Scampton. A second pilot in a two-seater plane was to accompany McConnell and bring him back after the plane had been delivered.

At 11:00 A.M. McConnell told his roommate, Lieutenant Larken, that he had to deliver an airplane to Tadcaster but that he expected to be back that same afternoon.

Normally the sixty-mile flight was routine; however, on that day McConnell and the second pilot ran into heavy fog. The second pilot made an emergency landing, but McConnell continued on to Tadcaster, though very much behind schedule. When he reached the field he started his approach for landing at a bad angle and crashed. Witnesses rushed to the crash scene and found the pilot dead. His watch had been broken at the time of the impact and had stopped at exactly 3:25 P.M.

At about that same moment Larkin was sitting in the room he shared with McConnell at Scampton. He heard footsteps coming up the corridor and heard the door open behind him. Then he heard the familiar words, "Hullo, boy!" This was McConnell's customary greeting. He turned around and saw the figure of McConnell, or what he took to be McConnell, standing in the doorway.

To Larkin there seemed nothing odd about McConnell's coming in at that moment. He said "Hullo! Back already?" The figure replied, "Yes. Got there all right. Had a good trip." The figure then said, "Well cheerio!" and went out, closing the door behind him.

About a quarter of an hour later another officer came into the room and Larkin told him that he had just seen McConnell.

It wasn't until dinner that evening that Larkin heard of McConnell's death. At first he assumed that McConnell had returned to Scampton, then gone out on another flight and been killed. It was hours before he fully realized that McConnell had been killed at almost exactly the same moment that he had seen the figure of McConnell standing in the door and had talked to that figure.

Larkin was a clearheaded young man who was skeptical about ghosts. He had no idea what had happened, but about two weeks later he wrote down a matter-of-fact account of the experience for McConnell's parents.

This account came to the attention of the British Society for Psychical Research (SPR), the country's foremost organization for investigating such matters. They questioned Larkin, and everybody else who had been involved. All the witnesses appeared to be extremely reliable.

The investigators considered all possible explanations, including the possibility of a hoax. Hoaxes are all too common in cases of this sort. But this would have involved an officer making up a story about the death of a fellow officer and, while fraud cannot be ruled out, the possibility seems highly unlikely.

In the end the investigators could come to no final conclusions. The case remains one of the most impressive, and puzzling, examples of a crisis apparition on record.

# COMMANDER POTTER'S VISION

During World War II, Wing Commander George Potter of the RAF was one of a group of British airmen stationed in Egypt. It was the job of these men to bomb German ships bringing supplies to the German troops in North Africa. The missions were flown mostly at night and were very dangerous.

One evening Commander Potter and his friend Reg Lamb were in the officers' room having a drink. Another group of officers sat nearby. Among them was another wing commander called Roy. The group Roy was with suddenly burst out laughing, as if someone had just told a joke. Potter turned toward the noise, but what he saw was totally unexpected and terrifying.

He saw Roy's head and shoulders moving slowly in what looked like a bottomless depth of blue-blackness.

His lips were drawn back from his teeth in a dreadful grin; he had eye sockets but no eyes; the remaining flesh of his face was blotched with greenish purple shadows.

Reg Lamb began tugging at his companion's sleeve. "What's the matter? You've gone white as a sheet ... as if you've seen a ghost."

"I have seen a ghost," said Potter. "It's Roy. Roy has the mark of death on him!"

Lamb saw nothing unusual, but Potter was still shaking. He knew that Roy was scheduled to be flying the next evening. He thought of asking that Roy be taken off the mission, but such a request would certainly be denied. In the end he decided that there was nothing he could do.

The following night Potter got the message that he had been fearing and expecting. Roy and his crew had been shot down and forced to ditch in the ocean. But there was still some hope. Another plane had seen the men climbing into a life raft.

Potter told himself that the men would be rescued and his vision of death would be proved wrong. But as the hours dragged on there was no sign of Roy and his crew.

"And then I knew what I had seen," said Potter. "The blue-black nothingness was the Mediterranean at night and Roy was floating somewhere in it dead, with just his head and shoulders held up by his life jacket."

# "BEWARE JACK"

Danton Walker was a Broadway columnist who was very popular during the 1940s and 1950s. He was also very interested in ghosts, and his columns and books were not only filled with tales of celebrities but also of ghostly encounters.

One story was told to him by an artist named Buell Mullen. She was visiting the summer home of her friend, Celeste McVoy Holden, at Penwater, on Lake Michigan, north of Grand Rapids. The house was large, rambling, and quite isolated.

Mrs. Holden, her four-month-old daughter, and a nurse were the only people who lived in the house. Some servants lived in the nearby town, but only came in during the day. Mrs. Holden had just been through a very nasty divorce from her husband, an unfriendly and often violent man.

Mrs. Mullen was expecting her husband to join them at Penwater. She was writing him a note explaining how to get to the place from Chicago. Suddenly "something" took control of her hand and she wrote the words "beware ... beware ... Jack."

She showed the writing to Mrs. Holden, who became pale. "Jack" was her former husband's name.

The two women decided to try and get a more complete message through the use of a Ouija board.

The message the board spelled out was "murder ... you and the child ... beware."

Mrs. Holden asked the board, "Shall we call the police?"

The board's response was "No ... useless ... prepare."

The women prepared as best they could. They went to what seemed like the safest section of the house and barricaded all the doors. Then they sat down to await developments.

When morning came and nothing happened they felt rather foolish, and had a good laugh themselves.

A few days later the laughing stopped. Mrs. Holden had a phone call from her cousin who lived in nearby Harbor Point.

"We were having a dance up here at Harbor Point the night before last," he said. "Jack came in, roaring drunk and waving a gun. He kept saying that he was going to kill you and the baby, too. We managed to keep him out of trouble and he left the Point at three in the morning."

Mrs. Holden never saw her former husband again. She learned that he had been confined to a mental institution because of his uncontrollable rages. He died about ten years later.

# VI.

# Ghostly Phenomena

# CHINA'S WALKING CORPSES

In China an unburied corpse was regarded as a potential danger, for the corpse was like an empty house. The air was thought to be full of invisible and mostly evil spirits and demons that might take possession of the corpse and turn into a monstrous being called a *Ch'iang Shich*. This popular tale of such a being is typical of many:

Very late one night four exhausted travelers arrived at an inn near the city of Shantung. The innkeeper told them there was no room available, but the travelers pleaded that they were too weary to go on. Finally the innkeeper agreed to put them up in a little shack some distance from the inn. But he did not tell them that his daughter-in-law had just died, and her unburied corpse was stretched out on a plank just behind a curtain in the shack.

Three of the travelers fell asleep immediately. The fourth, sensing some unknown danger, remained awake. To his horror he saw a bony hand pull the curtain aside, and he watched the greenish, glowing-eyed corpse emerge. The creature bent down over the sleeping men one by one and breathed on them. The foul breath from such a monster causes instant death. When the creature approached the only traveler who was awake, he was paralyzed with fear. Pretending to be asleep, he held his breath while the thing bent over him, and thus his life was saved. When the corpse returned to its place behind the curtain, the man bolted for the door and ran out into the night. The *Ch'iang Shich* heard the door open and ran after him.

The fleeing man could see the blazing eyes of the corpse behind him, and he knew it was gaining on him. He ducked behind a huge willow tree to hide, and as he peered cautiously around the trunk of the tree, he found himself staring directly into the burning eyes of the creature no more than a few feet away. The thing let out a hideous shriek and made a leap toward him. That was just too much for the poor man, who fell into a dead faint. In so doing his life was spared, for the corpse missed him completely and plunged forward with such force that it hit the tree and buried its long nails deep into the wood.

The next morning the corpse, no longer animated, was found with its nails stuck in the tree trunk. The intended victim was on the ground, still unconscious, but alive.

# THE *PALATINE* LIGHT

In 1752 the ship *Palatine* left Holland for America. It was packed with immigrants who hoped to start a new life in Philadelphia. But a storm blew her off course, and the crew mutinied. The terrified passengers were totally helpless for days.

Two days after Christmas the luckless ship ran aground on the rocks near Block Island, off the coast of Rhode Island. When the storm abated, local fishermen removed the surviving passengers. But then they attacked and looted the wreck.

After they had stripped the *Palatine* of everything of value, the fishermen set her afire and watched her drift out into the open sea. It was only then that they realized that not everyone had been taken off the ship. A woman, terrified and driven half-mad by the hardships she had endured, had hidden somewhere on the ship. Now she appeared from her hiding place. The fishermen watched in horror as she stood screaming on the deck until the flames consumed her.

Ever since then visitors to Block Island have reported the sight of what appears to be a burning ship just offshore. Locally this phenomenon is known as the *Palatine* light.

# THE SCREAMING WOMAN

From time to time, people who live along the Mississippi River near Vicksburg, Mississippi, have reported hearing the screams of a woman, coming from somewhere out in the river. The screams are usually followed by words in French: *"Aidez-moi au nom de Dieu, les hommes me blessent!"* Translated that means "Help me in the name of God, the men are hurting me!" No source for these mysterious screams has ever been found.

This particular phenomenon appears to have begun around the year 1875. Those along the river have linked the screams to something that occurred in June 1874. The riverboat *Iron Mountain* set out from Vicksburg for New Orleans carrying fifty-seven passengers and towing a string of barges. Somewhere on the voyage the big paddle wheel steamer disappeared. The barges were later found drifting in the river. The towropes had been slashed, not broken. Hundreds of miles of river bottom were dragged, but no trace of the *Iron Mountain* was ever located.

One of the most plausible explanations offered for the disappearance was that the ship was attacked by river pirates, who still operated quite freely for years after the Civil War. The *Iron Mountain* would have offered a tempting target to the pirates.

On the passenger list were several Creole woman who spoke French. Could the ghostly voice be that of one of the pirates' victims?

# THE VERSAILLES ADVENTURE

Have you ever had the feeling while visiting some old house or ancient monument that you had stepped into the past? Generally such a feeling is only a temporary one. But in 1901 two very respectable Englishwomen came to believe that they actually had stepped into the past. Their "adventure" is one of the most unusual and fascinating episodes in the history of psychic research.

On August 10, 1901, Ann Moberly and Eleanor Jourdain, who were touring France, visited the great palace of Versailles outside of Paris. Both women were teachers, intelligent and well educated, but neither had any particular interest in French history in general or Versailles in particular. Nor were they interested in ghosts. They were just ordinary tourists.

The pair was strolling toward a small palace on the grounds called the Petit Trianon. The Petit Trianon had been a favorite of the unfortunate Queen Marie Antoinette, who had been beheaded during the French Revolution.

The women went through a small gate, and suddenly everything seemed to change. The atmosphere became oppressive and the gardens around them looked unreal. They met two men who were wearing long green coats that looked like official uniforms. They came upon a dark, pockmarked man wearing a wide-brimmed hat and heavy cloak. The expression on his face was "very evil."

They saw "a young girl standing in a doorway who wore a white kerchief dress down to her ankles"; there was a lady sketching and finally when they came to a country house a young man offered to show them around to the front of the house. When they arrived there, they felt that they had returned to the twentieth century.

The two women agreed that something strange had happened, but they decided not to talk about it, but to write separate accounts and compare them. The written accounts were very similar, and they decided to do some research on Versailles.

Over the next two years the women came to the conclusion that they had stepped back into the past at a period shortly before the French Revolution overwhelmed King Louis XVI and Queen Marie Antoinette. They thought they could identify the pockmarked man as the queen's friend Comte de Vaudreuil, who was often at the palace. The woman who was sketching they identified as the queen herself. They determined the date upon which they had entered the past as August 5, 1789.

Three years later the two women again visited Versailles. Nothing was the same. "The commonplace, unhistorical atmosphere was totally inconsistent with the air of silent mystery by which we had been so much oppressed."

The two women wrote up their Versailles experience in a book called *An Adventure,* which became quite popular. The major reason that this case has been taken so seriously, is the very high caliber of the witnesses. Everyone, including hardened skeptics, has assumed that the women were telling what they believed to be the truth. Neither sought money or fame from her experience. There has never been a hint that either woman was an habitual liar or in any way mentally unbalanced. They were just as puzzled about what they had experienced as everyone else.

Today most observers would probably put the entire wonderful Versailles adventure down to a combination of mistaken identity, overactive imagination, and selective memory. But the story continues to be told and retold, perhaps because the notion that we can, somehow, step through a door to the past is such a very attractive and exciting one.

# SCREAMING SKULLS

Scattered throughout the British Isles are several so-called "screaming skulls." That is, skulls that, according to tradition, protest loudly if they are moved from their accustomed place.

The most celebrated of these grisly artifacts resides at Wardly Hall. It allegedly belonged to Roger Downes, a seventeenth century rake who had his head cut off during a drunken brawl on London Bridge. The head was sent off to his sister, who lived on the family estate of Wardly Hall in Manchester. His sister kept it, and though it has now been reduced to a skull, it is still there, and stoutly resists efforts to move it anywhere else.

In a book called *Traditions of Lancashire,* the author states: "The skull was removed secretly at first, but it invariably returned to the Hall and no human power could drive it hence. It has been riven to pieces, burnt and otherwise destroyed but on the subsequent day it was seen filling its wonted place." That is a little locked recess behind the main stairs. The Wardly Hall skull doesn't do a lot of screaming, but when it is moved it does appear to trigger storms.

Wrote one witness to an attempt to remove the skull: "The night but one following, such a storm arose about the house of wind and lightning as tore down some trees. When hearing of this my father went over to see the wreckage the storm had made."

The skull kept at a farmhouse in Dorsetshire actually does scream or at least make noise. There is considerable dispute as to whose skull it may be. Attempts to bury it resulted in terrible screams from the grave and ominous creaks and rattles in the house from which it has been removed.

At Turnstead Farm in Derbyshire there is a skull that has acquired the title of "Dickie." According to the most popular legend the skull is that of a murdered woman. Others say it is the skull of a murdered man named Ned Dixon. One observer wrote, "Twice within the memory of man, the skull has been taken from the premises; once on building the present house on the site of the old one, and another time, when an attempt was made to bury it in the Chapel churchyard. But there was no peace, no rest! It had to be replaced."

Local legend holds that Dickie's powers caused an entire rail line to be relocated in 1883. A bridge for a rail line between London and Manchester was being built in what was considered to be "Dickie's Territory," that is near the farmhouse in which the skull was kept. But the foundations for the bridge could never be properly laid owing to the boggy nature of the soil, and the line had to be diverted. The locals assumed that Dickie just didn't want those noisy trains rumbling by and disturbing her.

# CORDER'S SKULL

In 1826 an English countryman named William Corder killed his intended bride Maria Marten, and buried her body in the dirt floor of a structure called the Red Barn. It was a tawdry crime and Corder was a stupid and uninteresting murderer. He was quickly caught, convicted, and hanged. Yet for some reason the case called Murder in the Red Barn attracted an enormous amount of attention.

When Corder was hanged outside the gates of Bury St. Edmunds jail on August 11, 1828, there was a huge crowd on hand to witness the spectacle. After the hanging the executioner picked up a little extra money by selling pieces of the rope to members of the crowd.

Corder's body was sent to a medical school for dissection, a common fate for the corpses of the condemned at the time. Corder's skeleton was used for teaching anatomy. However, one of the hospital staff, a Dr. Kilner, stole the murderer's skull from the anatomy lab and put a spare skull atop the skeleton. He then had Corder's skull polished and placed in a fancy wooden box as a display in his drawing room.

The skull apparently was not happy about this treatment. Almost immediately hammering and sobbing sounds were heard coming from the box. Doors opened and then were slammed mysteriously. The servants reported that a odd-looking man had visited the house several times asking for the doctor, but he always vanished before anyone could get a good look at him.

Dr. Kilner tried to ignore these ominous happenings. Then one night there was an explosion in his drawing room. The doctor rushed into the room to see what had happened and was met with a blast of icy air. The candle he was carrying was blown out. He lit a match and the first thing he saw was the skull on the floor grinning at him. Around it lay the fragments of the box in which it had been kept.

That was enough for the doctor. He passed the ghastly relic on to F.C. Hopkins, a retired prison official who had collected a number of artifacts from the murder in the Red Barn. As Hopkins was taking the skull home he tripped. The skull fell out of the handkerchief in which he was carrying it and rolled past a lady, who promptly fainted.

Both Hopkins and Dr. Kilner had bad luck, and within months both were bankrupt. Naturally they blamed Corder's skull. Hopkins bribed a gravedigger to bury the skull in consecrated ground. After that the run of bad luck ceased, for the murderer's skull was apparently satisfied at last.

# GHOSTLY FOOTSTEPS

Among the most commonly reported ghostly phenomena are footsteps, usually heard in a darkened corridor at night. But Capt. A.W. Monckton had a more unusual experience with ghostly footsteps. When he was a magistrate in New Guinea he was staying alone in a house belonging to a friend. He was working on his official business when suddenly he realized that the doors leading to a veranda which had been closed were now open. In his book *Some Experiences of a New Guinea Resident Magistrate* he recounted:

"I became conscious that both doors were wide open and—hardly thinking what I was doing—I got up, closed them both and went on writing. A few minutes later I heard footsteps upon the coral path leading up to the house; they came across the squeaky palm veranda, my door opened, and the footsteps went across the room and—as I raised my eyes from my dispatch—the other door opened, and the footsteps passed across the veranda and down again on to the coral."

A short time later the experience was repeated. "... the squeak changed to the tramp of booted feet on the boarded floor. As I looked to see who it was, the tramp passed close behind my chair and across the room to the door, which opened, and then the tramp changed to the squeak and the squeak to the crash of the coral."

The most remarkable part of Monckton's experience came the third time the footsteps were heard. Monckton had brought in several of the servants in a futile attempt to locate the source of the sounds. They were all in the room when the footsteps passed through. "Precisely in the same manner came the tread of a heavily booted man, and then went out to the palm veranda where—in the now brilliant illumination—we could see the depressing at the spots from which the sound came, as though a man were stepping there."

## SUMMONING A SPIRIT

Calling up a spirit of the dead is a traditional magical operation. The best and most complete description of how this is done comes from the nineteenth century French magician and occultist Eliphas Levi.

In 1854, when Levi was in London, he attempted to summon the spirit of the ancient magician Apollonius of Tyana. Levi prepared himself by fasting for twenty-one days. He was alone when the ceremony was performed, so we have only his word for what happened.

The ceremonial room had four concave mirrors and an altar covered with white lambskin. A five-pointed star or pentagram was carved on top of the altar. There were two chafing dishes, one on the altar, the other on a tripod. Levi wore a white robe. All this white was to indicate that the magician was practicing white as opposed to black magic. On the magician's head was a wreath of vervain leaves, useful in warding off any demons that might accidentally be called up. In one hand the magician held a sword, in the other a copy of the ritual.

Fires were lit in the chafing dishes, and Levi began to chant a long incantation. As the chant rose in pitch, Levi felt the ground shake and he thought he saw a figure of a man standing before the altar, but the figure vanished.

The magician repeated the incantations, and this time something seemed to stir in the depths of the mirrors. Levi closed his eyes and summoned three times for the ghost to appear. "When I again looked forth there was a man in front of me, wrapped from head to foot in a species of shroud, which seemed more grey than white, he was lean, melancholy and beardless."

Levi suddenly felt abnormally cold and badly frightened. He tried to command the spirit but was unable to speak properly. Something touched his sword arm, which went numb at the elbow. He was overcome by intense weakness and he fainted.

For several days after the ceremony, Levi's arm was sore. The questions he had intended to ask the ghost had never been asked, though Levi felt that they had been answered in his mind. The answers were "death" and "dead." The magician did not reveal the questions.

Levi never said that he actually saw the ghost. But then he never said that it was all an hallucination either. He did, however, warn anyone attempting such a ceremony that the result is "intense exhaustion and frequently a shock sufficient to occasion illness."

# SPOOK LIGHTS

Throughout the United States there are various places where mysterious lights appear regularly. Generally local tradition gives these lights a ghostly origin. One of the best-known of the "spook lights" is in the West Mountain Valley area of Colorado, where the lights appear, appropriately enough, over a graveyard. The graveyard is just outside of the town of Silver Cliff, once a prosperous mining town but now—again appropriately—a ghost town, with a tiny population.

The strange phenomenon of the lights was first observed in about 1880, when Silver Cliff was at its boomtown height, with a population of about five thousand. A group of drunken miners returning from their diggings reported seeing eerie lights hovering over each grave in the local graveyard. Drunken miners do not make the most reliable witnesses, but other more reliable and completely sober observers began seeing the lights, too. The lights continued to be seen over the years, and in 1967 a story about them appeared in the *New York Times*. The lights became something of a tourist attraction. The most complete account of the lights appeared in the *National Geographic* magazine in 1969.

Author Edward J. Linehan described them as "dim round spots of blue-white light" glowing over the graves. As he approached they vanished, but slowly reappeared.

One popular theory was that the lights were merely a reflection of lights from Silver Cliff and another nearby small town. Linehan thought the lights from the towns were too faint to cause such an effect, and he noted they were often seen when the fog was so thick that you couldn't see the town at all. Another theory is that they are caused by radioactive ore, but no unusual levels of radioactivity were found.

Linehan cited the theory of anthropologist and folklorist Dale Ferguson that the Cheyenne and other Plains Indians buried their dead on "hilltops sacred to the spirits." A number of Native American legends speak of "dancing blue spirits" on such sites.

Old-timers in the Silver Cliff area have another explanation; they will tell you that the lights are the helmet lamps of long-dead miners still searching for silver on the hilltops.

# THE OUIJA BOARD

Many methods have been devised to try to communicate with the dead. Far and away the most popular is the Ouija board. The name comes from the French *Oui* and the German *Ja,* two words that mean yes.

The original Ouija board consisted of thirty-eight cards ranged around the edge of a polished table. On twenty-six of the cards are the letters of the alphabet, on ten of them the numbers 0 to 9, and on the last two the words Yes and No. Those taking part then sit around the table and place their index fingers on an ordinary overturned drinking glass. A question is asked. The glass then moves toward either the Yes or No card, or it may move toward the letters and numbers spelling out the answer.

Today this type of Ouija has been almost entirely replaced by a commercially produced board. It is made of a highly polished wood and contains the letters, numbers, and Yes and No of the original version.

Instead of a glass the modern Ouija board uses a planchette (named after its French inventor in 1835), a heart-shaped piece of wood with three legs. The function of the planchette has changed since it was first developed. Originally it had two small wheels with a pencil providing the third leg of support. One person would place his or her hand on the planchette and, if the conditions were favorable, it would move about, writing messages on a piece of paper with the pencil. With the Ouija board people place their fingertips on the planchette and it slides over the board pointing to the letters and numbers in response to questions. The theory is that the planchette is moved by the spirits, or at least by some sort of outside force.

The problem with the Ouija board is that the planchette or the glass can be moved by the slightest pressure. It can be moved even if the person actually applying the pressure is unaware of what he or she is doing. This has been demonstrated in many experiments. It is absolutely impossible to know whether the "message" that the board appears to be delivering comes from some outside force, or from one of those who fingers are on the glass or planchette.

Today there are still some who take the Ouija seriously. Others believe that it is dangerous because the messages may come from diabolical sources. Most people, however, regard it as little more than a game. Indeed, the best-selling Ouija board is manufactured by one of the world's largest manufacturers of parlor games.

# BURIED ALIVE

The fear of being buried alive is an ancient and deep-seated one. Today with modern medical technology the possibility of being prematurely buried is virtually non-existent. But in past centuries the possibility of falling into an unconscious and deathlike state and being buried or placed in a crypt only to revive when it was too late, while remote, certainly existed. This would be particularly true during times of epidemic, when there were lots of deaths and a big hurry to get the bodies underground and out of the way. This fear haunted the nightmares of many writers, in particular, Edgar Allan Poe, who wrote several stories on the theme.

Along with numerous accounts of people who had been buried and then dug up and found to be still alive, there are those tales that have a more ghostly element. This one is typical:

A man named Samuel Jocelyn of North Carolina was thrown from his horse, struck his head on a rock, and was pronounced dead by the local doctor and quickly buried.

A few nights after the funeral Jocelyn's old friend Alexander Hostler was troubled by a bad dream. In the dream the form of his friend Jocelyn appeared before him.

"How could you let me be buried when I was not dead?" asked the shade of Jocelyn.

"But you were dead," insisted Hostler.

"No I wasn't," replied the form. "Open my coffin and you will see that I am not lying the way I was buried."

Hostler tried to ignore the dream, but it kept coming back night after night. It seemed that he would continue to have the terrible dream until he did something about it. So he persuaded a friend to go with him at night to the graveyard and dig up Jocelyn's grave. When they opened the coffin lid, they found that though Jocelyn had been buried faceup, just like everyone else, the corpse was now facedown. Somehow it had turned over.

# THE PHANTOM FACES

In December 1924 there was an accident aboard the SS *Watertown,* an oil tanker owned by the Cities Service Company. The ship was en route to the Panama Canal from the Pacific Coast. Two merchant seamen, James Courtney and Thomas Meehan, were cleaning one of the cargo holds when they apparently were overcome by fumes and died. As was usual in such cases the bodies were buried at sea on December 4, 1924.

The very next day the first mate reported to the captain that the faces of the two dead men could be seen in the water and apparently were following the ship. Captain Keith Tracy looked out into the water and, sure enough, there were the faces of the dead men. The faces kept pace with the ship for several days and were seen by all of the officers and members of the crew repeatedly and for long periods of time.

After the ship made its way through the Panama Canal and docked at New Orleans the captain made a full report to the officials of the Cities Service Company. One company official suggested that if the faces should appear again they should be photographed. Captain Tracy was given a roll of sealed film, and observed while he loaded it into a camera. This was a precaution to prevent fraud.

On the return voyage six photographs were taken. They were not developed until the *Watertown* once again docked at New Orleans. Five of the photos showed nothing, the sixth clearly showed faces in the water.

While a blowup of the photograph was put on display at the Cities Services offices in New York, the story was not published until 1934. By that time some of the crewmen from the *Watertown* had died, and others were impossible to locate.

The details of how the photographs were taken and developed remains unknown, although apparently Captain Tracy and his assistant engineer had sworn to their authenticity. The photos had also been checked for tampering by a detective agency. The original negatives were returned to Cities Service, and lost.

This case remains a unique and intriguing one.

# BLACK AGGIE

Here is a scene you have probably seen in a dozen films about the supernatural: It is midnight in the graveyard. A mist rises. The clock strikes twelve. As the camera pans over the tombstones it lingers on one monument, a tombstone with a carved angel on top. Suddenly the eyes of the statue begin to glow with an evil light.

This is just what is supposed to have happened at a cemetery outside of Baltimore, Maryland. The "haunted tombstone" marks the grave of newspaper publisher General Felix Angus, who died in the 1920s. His tombstone had a curious-looking angel carved from black stone perched on top.

The monument acquired the name Black Aggie and a sinister reputation. A belief grew that at midnight Black Aggie's eyes would glow. It was also said that anyone who was struck by the angel's glowing gaze would immediately go blind. Pregnant women who passed under her shadow, where no grass would ever grow, would have miscarriages.

It was also rumored that the tombstone had become part of the initiation rites of a local college fraternity, which required that a prospective member had to spend the entire night sitting beneath (or on) Black Aggie. However, the first candidate to try was found dead the next morning. The cause of death was fright, and the case was hushed up by the college.

This sort of reputation is rarely good for a monument. In 1962 one of Black Aggie's arms disappeared. It later turned up in the trunk of a car along with a strong saw. The owner of the car claimed that Black Aggie had sawed off her own arm and given it to him. An ingenious defense, but it didn't work. He was sent to jail anyway.

Black Aggie had become so notorious that tourists would gather in the cemetery at night to see if they could catch a glimpse of her glowing eyes. The fear of blindness did not worry them. But the Angus family worried about further desecrations to the grave. In 1967 Black Aggie was removed from the tombstone and donated to the Smithsonian Institution, where she is gathering dust in some storeroom. She has never been put on display.

# THE PHANTOM BUS

During the early 1930s there were tales of a phantom bus in London. It would appear in the most alarming possible way. A driver would be coming along St. Mark's Road, just minding his own business, when suddenly he would see this gigantic red double-decker bus rushing toward him. By the time he saw the bus there was absolutely nothing that could be done. All the terrified driver could do was hit the brakes, wait for the crash, and pray—if he was a praying man.

It is possible that some nonbelievers became instant converts to the power of prayer, for there was no crash. The bus simply disappeared. The phantom bus caused a couple of minor accidents, when drivers swerved to get out of its way.

None of the accidents caused by the sighting of the phantom bus was serious until June 11, 1933. Then a driver swerved and crashed head-on into another car. The driver of the second car was killed. After that there were no more sightings of the ghost bus. Perhaps its obscure but deadly mission had finally been fulfilled after it claimed a victim.

# THE HAIRY HANDS

There is a stretch of road in the English county of Devon that is supposed to be haunted by something called The Hairy Hands. The road near the town of Postbridge appears to have had more than its share of unexplained accidents.

The road's reputation as a dangerous place began back in the days of the horse and carriage. Drivers said that sometimes their horses would veer off suddenly, for no apparent reason. More than one carriage was left overturned in the ditch.

Later, when the road was modernized for automobiles, matters grew even worse. Those who seemed to suffer most severely were motorcyclists. There were several fatal accidents where the motorcycles seemed to have been ridden right off the road. Those who survived the accidents often reported that it felt as though something had taken control of their motorcycles and literally forced them off the road. And there were even more dramatic accounts, like this one:

"A young man, a guest at Penlee in Postbridge, undertook to run in to Princetown on his motor bicycle to get something for his hostess. In about an hour he returned to Penlee, very white and shaken, and saying he had had a most curious experience. He said he had felt his hands gripped by two rough hairy hands and every effort made to throw him off the machine."

After a couple of similar accounts The Hairy Hands became national news in England. Reporters managed to dig up other stories, including a very dramatic one from a couple who had once camped in the area:

"It was a cold moonlit night and I was in my bunk in a caravan [trailer] ... I was at the side of the caravan facing a small window at the end, under which my husband lay deeply asleep in his bunk. I awoke suddenly with a feeling of fear and danger, and quite wide awake. I knew there was some power very seriously menacing us near, and I must act swiftly. As I at last looked up to the little window at the end of the caravan I saw something moving, and as I stared, my heart beating fast, I saw it was the fingers and palm of a very large hand with many hairs on the joints and back of it, clawing up to the top of the window which was a little open ... I knew that the owner of the hand hated us and wished us harm, and I knew it was no ordinary human hand and that no blow or shot would have any power over it."

Fortunately the hand disappeared before actually doing anything.

More mundane explanations for the problems on the road came from engineers who said that there was something wrong with the way the road was constructed, and that is why there were so many accidents. The road was actually resurfaced, but to no avail.

In recent years, however, encounters with The Hairy Hands seem to have become less frequent.

# THE RETURN FLIGHT

During World War II Captain Charles "Brick" Barton was pilot of a B-24 that carried out bombing missions over Germany in the spring of 1943. The raids were extremely dangerous. Though Barton himself had never been wounded, his plane had been hit several different times. His veteran copilot was hurt in one of the missions, so when Barton's B-24 took off again his copilot was a young lieutenant on his first combat mission. The target was a difficult and well-defended one.

After the plane had dropped its bombs and headed for home it was struck by machine gun fire from a German pursuit plane. Barton was hit, his blood splattered all over the instrument panel and around the cabin. The machine gun fire had also damaged the plane's controls. It was flyable but difficult to handle.

The young and inexperienced copilot was forced to

take over the controls, and he very nearly panicked. Then he heard Barton's calm and reassuring voice telling him exactly what to do. The captain had clearly been badly injured, but he refused to be taken into the back of the plane, where he might have been made more comfortable. The copilot marveled at how clearheaded and in control Barton was for a man who must have been in great pain and had lost a lot of blood.

The copilot, guided by the instructions of the wounded veteran, kept the plane on course for its flight back to England, which took over an hour.

As they neared home base the copilot radioed for an ambulance. Barton had suddenly fallen silent for the first time during the return flight. The lieutenant feared that he had become unconscious from loss of blood.

The young man brought the balky plane down for a safe landing. The flight surgeon was waiting for him.

The lieutenant fended off all congratulations, saying that if it had not been for Barton's instructions he never would have made it. "He's the real hero."

The flight surgeon climbed into the plane, and a short time later came out looking grim. He took the young man aside and asked him if he was sure about having talked to Captain Barton during the return flight.

"Of course I'm sure," said the young man. "I told you we never would have been able to make it back if it hadn't been for his help."

"That's impossible," said the ashen-faced surgeon, "Captain Barton was shot in the head. He must have died instantly, and he's been dead for over an hour."

# THE TULIP STAIRCASE

In 1966 two Canadian tourists, the Reverend Ralph Hardy, a retired clergyman, and his wife were visiting the National Maritime Museum in Greenwich, England.

One of the buildings on the museum grounds is the Queen's House, built for Anne of Denmark, wife of King James I. Inside the Queen's House is a fine spiral staircase called the Tulip Staircase. The Reverend Hardy took a picture of it. The staircase was empty when the shot was taken.

After the Reverend Hardy returned to Canada and had the picture developed he found that it contained an image of what appeared to be a robed figure climbing the stairs. The figure's left hand, with a ring, can clearly be seen holding the handrail. Some people think that they can even see a second or third robed figure in the picture.

The Reverend Hardy and his wife had never been interested in ghosts, and everyone who interviewed them was absolutely convinced that they were not the sort of people to fake ghost photographs.

The Queen's House and the Tulip Staircase never had a reputation for being haunted before the photograph was taken and given wide publicity. Afterward, of course, a number of people said that they, too, had seen ghostly robed figures on or near the staircase. Such stories are not taken seriously. The photograph, however, remains a mystery.

# PHONE CALL FROM THE DEAD

Don Owens of Toledo, Ohio, had a close friend named Lee Epps. Epps, who lived alone, was basically a shy and lonely man. He was very attached to Owens, and his wife Ethyl, whom he called "Sis."

On the evening of October 28, 1968, the phone rang at the Owens's house. Don Owens was out, but his wife recognized Epps's voice immediately. He sounded urgent, and the message was upsetting:

"Sis, tell Don I'm feeling real bad. Never felt this way before. Tell him to get in touch with me the minute he comes in. It's important, Sis."

When Don Owens returned he tried to call his friend. There was no answer. Later that night he learned that Lee Epps had been in the hospital just a few blocks from where the Owens family lived. He had been in a deep coma. He died at 10:30 P.M., the very time the phone call had come in. Doctors agree that there was no way that Epps could have regained consciousness and made the phone call before he died.

That is just one of many reports of phone calls coming from someone who had just died, or has been long dead. Here is another case:

A young man named Karl had lived with his grandmother while he was growing up. The old lady was almost completely deaf. When Karl went out, and his grandmother was to be alone, he would leave her with a telephone number where he could be reached.

If she wanted him, she would dial the number and say, "This is Karl's grandmother. Would you tell him that I need him home?" The grandmother was so deaf that she couldn't hear if anybody answered the phone or not. She would just repeat the phrase five or six times and hang up.

Karl's grandmother died when he was about sixteen. Two years later he was at the home of his friend Peter. Peter and his family didn't know anything about the old woman's strange way of making calls.

Karl and Peter were in the basement when the phone rang upstairs. Peter's mother answered. Then she shouted to the basement:

"Karl, there's an old woman on the phone. She says she's your grandmother and she says she needs you. She just keeps saying it over and over again."

Karl rushed up the stairs and grabbed the phone. But the line was dead.

# HITCHCOCK'S FAVORITE GHOST STORY

Alfred Hitchcock, the master of mystery and suspense films, had a real ghost story that he considered one of the greatest mysteries of all time.

The event took place in January 1934. Twenty-year-old Arnie Gandy's parents knew that he was in San Francisco. They were expecting a call from him. So when the phone rang in their New York apartment at 3:00 A.M. they were not too surprised. It would only be midnight in California.

The voice Arnie's mother heard was not one that she recognized.

"The kid is here and for God's sake forgive him and give him another chance. What I said about him in my letter is all true. He's a fine kid."

Arnie's mother asked who was speaking, but the caller didn't give a name. She insisted it must be the wrong number, but the caller repeated the number and it was correct—and their phone number was unlisted.

She asked to talk to her boy. The caller replied:

"Your son is in a hospital in San Francisco. He's in bad shape, but never mind. He's on his way home now."

There was the sound of other voices in the room, and some laughter. Then another voice—which sounded like Arnie's said:

"I'm helpless. Here I lie propped up on pillows. I can't move." There was a groan and the line went dead.

Arnie's frantic mother contacted the operator, who assured her that the call had come from San Francisco. Arnie's father called the police, who were unable to trace the call.

The next morning Arnie Gandy's body was found in San Francisco Bay. He had been dead for at least two days—well before the mysterious phone call had been placed. The letter the mysterious caller said he had written never arrived.

There was a genuine mystery concerning the boy's death. He had signed onto a ship in New York as a mess boy for a world cruise. When the ship docked in San Francisco, Arnie went ashore and never returned. He did not take his clothes or any personal affects from the ship.

That same day he wrote a cheerful letter to his parents, with no indication anything was wrong. He was never seen again until his body was fished out of the water six days later.

Despite a careful investigation, there were no clues as to why Arnie Gandy left the ship, where he had spent his last days, whether his death was accident, suicide, or murder, or who had made the mysterious phone call.

Hitchcock commented, "If I made it into a movie, no one would believe it."

# VII.

# Ghostly Legends

# GHOSTS OF THE ANCIENT GREEKS

To the ancient Greeks ghosts were more to be pitied than feared. This attitude is expressed most clearly in Homer's *Odyssey*. When Odysseus asks how long it will be before he returns home from his wanderings, he is told that he must descend into the underworld and question the ghost or shade of the great prophet Tiresias.

As Odysseus descended into the gloomy twilight world, the phantoms of the dead crowded around him but were so weak and insubstantial that they hardly had enough strength to speak. Odysseus dug a pit and filled it with the blood of sacrificed animals, but he had to keep the ghosts at bay with his sword until the spirit of Tiresias appeared to drink first.

The lot of these shades in the underworld was a miserable one. The great hero Achilles, now a pale shade, informed Odysseus, "I had rather be a poor man's serf than king over all the dead."

But if the underworld was bad, the prospect of roaming the earth as a spirit was even worse. Not only were such spirits miserable, they were a potential danger to the living. Greek soldiers would sometimes cut the feet off the corpses of enemies they had slain in battle. The hope was that the crippled ghost would then be unable to pursue its killer effectively.

The best way to assure that the spirits of the dead

would rest easily and not return to trouble the living was to make sure that the body was properly buried. While in the underworld, Odysseus met the ghost of one of his own sailors who had been killed but had not been buried. The ghost warned Odysseus not to tempt the wrath of the gods by allowing his corpse to remain unburied.

The Greeks and many other ancient peoples would go to great lengths to make sure that their dead were properly interred. One of the greatest of all the Greek plays concerns the efforts of Antigone to obtain a proper burial for the remains of her brother. Even today the elaborate lengths to which people will go to recover the bodies of the dead can be traced back, at least in part, to the ancient fear that if a body lies unburied, its ghost may return to torment the living.

# THE *FLYING DUTCHMAN*

Of all the ghostly legends of the sea the best-known by far is the legend of the *Flying Dutchman*. No one seems to know where the legend began. An early version appeared in a British magazine in 1821, and that version formed the basis for a short story, a play, and a well-known opera.

In brief the legend is this: There is a ship sailing around the Cape of Good Hope, the southern tip of Africa, when it suddenly encounters a terrible storm.

The crew begs the captain to put into a safe harbor. Not only does the captain refuse, he mocks their fears and says that he is afraid of nothing on earth or in heaven. A glowing form appears on the deck, but the captain is still unafraid. He shouts, "Who wants a peaceful passage? I don't! I'm asking nothing from you." Then he draws his pistol and takes a shot at the form.

This is a fatal mistake. The pistol explodes in the captain's hand. The form then pronounces a curse on the captain. He is doomed to sail forever, without rest. "And since it is your delight to torment sailors you shall torment them, for you shall be the evil spirit of the sea. Your ship shall bring misfortune to all who sight it."

One possible origin of the *Flying Dutchman* legend may be in the exploits of a seventeenth century Dutch captain named Bernard Fokke. He was supposed to be a daring mariner whose voyages were so remarkable that it was rumored he had supernatural aid. Fokke's ship disappeared without a trace, and this may have strengthened the supernatural association.

While the *Flying Dutchman* legend has enjoyed a great literary popularity, it is difficult to determine just how widely believed the legend was among sailors. But sightings of the *Flying Dutchman*, or at least some phantom ship, have been reported by many experienced mariners.

Of all the reports, the best-known was that made in 1881 by the man who was to become King George V of England. He was serving aboard the *Bacchante* when in July:

"The *Flying Dutchman* crossed our bows. A strange red light appeared, as of a phantom ship all aglow, in the midst of which light the masts, spars and sails of a brig two hundred yards distant stood up in strong relief... On arriving there, no vestige nor any sign whatever of any material ship was to be seen either near or right away to the horizon, the night being clear, the sea calm. Thirteen persons altogether saw her."

Shortly after the encounter the first man to have sighted the phantom ship fell to his death from the mast. The admiral aboard the *Bacchante* became ill and died before the end of the voyage. The future king, however, appears to have suffered no ill effects from the encounter.

# THE DEMON LOVER

There is a bit of folk wisdom which holds that a person should not mourn too long or too deeply for a loved one who has died. The loud mourning, this legend holds, may attract the attention of an evil spirit, and this spirit may appear in the form of the dead lover, with terrible results. This is the legend of the demon lover, and it has been retold in many forms.

This version, from Germany, is one of the most common: There was a young farmer named Bruno who was rounded up and forced to serve in the army of the king of Prussia. He left behind a young woman named Lenore, whom he had promised to marry, and who loved him very much.

Months passed and word began to spread that the Prussian army had suffered a terrible defeat and many were killed. Slowly survivors began to straggle back home, but Bruno was not among them. Nor did anyone seem to know what had happened to him. Gradually Lenore began to realize that her love had died on some distant battlefield.

Lenore was overcome with grief. She shut herself up in her room and cried out either for Bruno's return or for her own death so that she could join him. Her family feared for her sanity.

Then one winter night she heard a horse gallop up in front of the house, and a familiar voice called her name. Lenore had the wild hope that Bruno somehow had not been killed, but had merely been taken prisoner, and now had returned.

She rushed out of the house, and there was Bruno, looking exactly as Lenore had remembered him, yet strangely changed. His movements were stiff and mechanical, and there was no expression on his face. He reached down and lifted the girl up behind him on the large black horse that he was riding.

The horse galloped through the village and onto the broad highway, its hooves barely touching the ground. Lenore was freezing, and she clung to her lover for warmth, but his body was as cold as the air around it.

The ride seemed to last for hours. Finally the black horse drew up in front of iron gates, which swung open as it approached. Lenore now realized that the horse had carried them to a graveyard.

The figure that she had taken to be Bruno dismounted and pulled her roughly to the ground. The figure had changed now. The uniform was rotted and tattered. The face had become a mask of skin tightly stretched over a grinning skull.

It pointed a skeletal hand to an open grave and said, "This is our wedding bed."

The next morning the caretaker of the cemetery found that an open grave had been filled in. He made no attempt to explore further, for he had long since come to the conclusion that to do so would simply stir up evil spirits.

# THE GHOSTLY WANDERER

History and legend are full of tales of individuals who have been forced to wander the earth for all eternity as a punishment for some terrible crime. There is a popular nineteenth century version of this story from New England.

It is contained in a letter from a man named William Austin. He said that in 1826 he was riding in a coach outside of Boston, when the coach encountered an open carriage driven by a man accompanied by a young girl. The carriage seemed to be pursued by rain clouds.

The driver of the coach said that this particular carriage had been seen by many people. The carriage driver often stopped to ask the way to Boston, but he never seemed to listen to the directions, and always started off the wrong way, muttering about how he had to get to the city by nightfall.

Three years later Austin saw the same carriage in Hartford, Connecticut, and learned that the driver's name was Peter Rugg. He actually stepped out into the road and waved down the carriage.

"Are you Peter Rugg?" he asked.

"My name is Peter Rugg," said the man. "I have unfortunately lost my way. Will you please direct me to Boston?"

Austin found out that Rugg lived on Middle Street in Boston, and was not quite sure how long he had been traveling. Both Rugg and the girl with him were wet, though the weather was clear. Rugg said they had been caught in a heavy shower up by the river. He refused to believe that he was in Connecticut, and insisted that he was only a short distance from Boston, and again drove off in the wrong direction.

When Austin visited Boston he was able to dig out more of the story. In about 1730 a man named Peter Rugg had lived on Middle Street. He was a stubborn man with a fierce temper and would take advice from no one. One autumn morning Rugg took his daughter for a drive to the town of Concord. On the way back he stopped at the house of a friend who warned him that a storm was approaching.

"Let the storm increase," swore Rugg. "I will see home tonight in spite of the storm, or may I never see home!"

With these words he whipped his horse and disappeared into the night. He did not get home that night or the next day or any other night. No trace of him or his daughter was ever found.

# TREGAGLE

There are many accounts of ghosts being called into court either to point out their murderers, explain how they wanted their property divided, or generally to clear up some business left unfinished during their lifetime.

But summoning a ghost for any purpose was always a dangerous business, as the story of Jan Tregagle amply demonstrates.

Tregagle was supposed to be a crooked lawyer who practiced in the western part of Cornwall in England during the late sixteenth or early seventeenth century. A man who lived in the county lent some money to another without receiving any security, or even a written acknowledgment of the loan. Tregagle was the sole witness to the transaction. However, the lawyer died before the money was repaid. Soon after Tregagle's death the lender demanded his money, and the debtor insisted he never received any money.

The case went to court. The lender said that Tregagle was the only witness. The debtor denied it, and with an oath swore, "If Tregagle ever saw it I wish to God that Tregagle may come and declare it."

With those words the ghost of Tregagle appeared. It pointed to the man and said, "I can no more be a false witness. Thou hast had the money and found it easy to bring me from the grave but thou will not find it so easy to put me away."

Wherever the terrified man moved about the court Tregagle followed him; he begged the judges to get rid of the spirit. "That's thy business," they sad. "Thou has brought him, thou may get rid of him."

The man returned home, but Tregagle pursued him. The ghost was always beside him, night and day. He repaid the borrowed money, gave money to the poor, and then tried to get rid of the spirit with the aid of the ministers in the area.

They attempted to "bind" the spirit—that is confine it to one place where it would not bother anyone. This was no easy task. Tregagle kept breaking free and returning to the poor tormented fellow who had so unwisely called him up in the first place. Finally it is said that the spirit was confined to the shore of Whitesand Bay, where on stormy days he can still be heard roaring in anger. In that part of Cornwall a howling wind is sometimes called a Tregagle.

# LADY HOWARD

There are certain notorious figures in history around whom ghostly legends tend to cluster. Such a figure is Lady Frances Howard, a celebrated beauty at the court of James I of England.

Lady Howard had four husbands and was reputed to

have poisoned two of them. Along with one of her husbands, she was sent to the Tower of London for the poisoning of Sir Thomas Overbury, in what was one of the most sensational murder cases of the time. Later she was released.

According to Dartmoor folklorist Ruth E. St. Leger-Gordon, "For all these crimes Lady Howard now pays a penalty after death. Every night, according to one version of the tale, she assumes the shape of a large black dog, in which guise she runs beside a coach of bones driven by a headless coachman. The goal of the expedition is Okehampton Casle ... Upon arrival she still in dog-guise, plucks one blade of grass which she carries in her mouth back to her old home site at Tavistock. When every blade of grass in the Castle grounds is removed in this way at a rate of one per night, the penance will be completed and the poor lady will be able to rest in peace. Judging by the amount of mowing still necessary around the ruins ... she has many more nocturnal journeys before her."

St. Leger-Gordon points out that Lady Frances Howard actually had no connection with Okehampton Castle. Okehampton once belonged to the family of Lady *Mary* Howard, a contemporary of, but no relation to, the notorious Lady Frances. The confusion of names and the universal desire to spin a good tale has consigned the perfectly innocent Lady Mary to a horrible and apparently eternal fate, at least in folklore.

# CHRISTMAS GHOSTS

Today ghosts are most closely associated with the night before All Saints' Day, All Hallows' Eve or Halloween. But traditionally ghosts were most closely associated with another holiday—Christmas. Indeed, Christmas is the only holiday which has its own separate literary genre—the Christmas ghost story. The most famous of all Christmas stories, *A Christmas Carol* by Charles Dickens, is a ghost story. Dickens subtitled the tale *A Ghost Story of Christmas.* He wrote:

"There is probably a smell of roasted chestnuts and other comfortable things all the time for we are telling Winter stories—Ghost stories—round the Christmas fire; and we have never stirred except to draw a little nearer to it."

We don't really know how or why the telling of ghost stories became associated with Christmas. In the days before television and electric lights sitting around the fire telling stories was a popular form of entertainment. Christmas comes at the darkest time of year, and ghost stories have always been popular.

The tradition was well established in England by the eighteenth century, but it was the publication of the enormously successful *Christmas Carol* that made a private practice a public one. Other writers began produc-

NEW YORK PUBLIC LIBRARY

*Marley's ghost from Charles Dickens's* A Christmas Carol, *one of the most beloved ghost stories in English literature.*

ing Christmas ghost stories, and though they did not necessarily concern Christmas, they were certainly ghost stories, and they appeared in magazines around Christmastime, presumably for reading and retelling during the holiday season.

By about 1860 the Christmas ghost story became a regular feature of Christmas Annuals published both in Britain and America. These were elaborately printed editions of popular magazines. They were expensive and frequently given as gifts. They contained games, plays, and more often than not at least one ghost story.

Not all Christmas ghost stories appeared in magazines. Many families had their own collections. One of the most celebrated personal collections was kept by Lord Halifax. Years later his son wrote of what Christmastime was like at his home:

"As long as I can remember, my father's Ghost Book was one of the most distinctive associations of Hickleton [the family home]. He kept it always with great care himself, from time to time making additions to it in his own hand-writing and bringing it out on special occasions such as Christmas to read some of the particular favorites aloud before we all went to bed . . .

"Such treatment of young nerves, even in those days, would not have been everybody's prescription; and I well recollect my mother protesting—though I think almost inevitably to no effect—against 'the children being frightened too much' . . . The victims themselves, fascinated and spell-bound by a sense of delicious terror, never failed to ask for more."

During the twentieth century the popularity of the Christmas Annual has faded, as has the custom of telling or reading ghost stories at Christmas—except of course

*A Christmas Carol.* The specters of Christmas have been almost entirely replaced by the jolly fat man in the red suit. But the era did leave behind a fine collection of supernatural tales.

# THE PHANTOM BRAKEMAN

Of all the ghostly legends attached to railroading, that of the phantom brakeman is probably the most widely told. Here is a version from usptate New York.

Chuck Tolley had been an itinerant brakeman on the railroad. He changed jobs often, and one night he was traveling to a new job. He was riding in the caboose, the last car of the train, where crewmen often stayed when they were off duty. Tolley was waiting for his friend, the regular brakeman on the run, to finish his inspection.

It was a terribly stormy evening, and it was the job of the brakeman to climb around the cars to make sure everything was in order. But the rain had weakened the roadbed, so that when the train hit a sharp curve the first dozen cars were derailed, and the brakeman was thrown from the top of the train. He landed between the cars and was beheaded. Tolley found his friend's body, but the head was never found.

Many men had lost their lives in similar accidents. Such dangers were simply part of trying to keep a railroad running in all kinds of weather. But the accident had a profound effect on Tolley. Once he thought he had all the time in the world; now he realized that the future was uncertain, and he began to think about settling down, getting married, and raising a family.

He took a regular job as a fireman and then became an engineer; the pay was much better and the work was more regular. Still he always tried to avoid assignments on the run where his friend had been killed. But he was assigned to the run anyway, and he knew it would do no good to object. Every time he came to the deadly curve he would slow down, especially in rainy weather.

He traveled the run for several years without incident. He was almost able to pass the scene of the accident without thinking about it—almost.

One rainy evening in March as he approached the fatal curve he saw a red warning light on the track ahead. He brought the train to a grinding, screeching halt and told the fireman to go up the line to investigate.

The fireman came back and said that nothing was wrong. Tolley was not satisfied, and though he knew it was not proper for an engineer to leave his train, he went to investigate himself.

Tolley saw a red light bobbing above the tracks. It seemed to be coming from an old-style red globe lantern, the type trainmen had used when he first started working on the railroad.

Tolley thought he could see the lower part of a man's body faintly illuminated in the glow. The body appeared to be wearing the regulation blue overalls of a brakeman.

Tolley raised his own lantern and saw, to his horror, that the figure in the blue overalls carrying the red lantern had no head!

Then the figure disappeared, but Tolley knew that the ghost he had seen was that of his old brakeman friend.

He also knew that the phantom had appeared for some reason. Tolley walked a little farther up the tracks and found that the rains had washed a large boulder down on the track. If the train had hit the boulder there would have been a terrible accident.

While the other members of the train crew were certainly glad to have avoided the accident, they simply laughed at Tolley's story of a headless brakeman.

However, Chuck Tolley knew what he had seen. He had been given a warning; he might not be given another.

The next morning he quit his job on the railroad.

# THE PHANTOM HITCHHIKER

Undoubtedly the most popular and widely told ghostly legend in America is that of the phantom hitchhiker. There are many variations but the basic story goes like this:

A young man is driving along a deserted road late one Saturday night. He stops to pick up a girl of about seventeen wearing a white dress who is hitchhiking toward the city. She gives him an address, and he agrees to drop her off. He offers the girl his jacket because she appears to be cold. She thanks him and climbs into the backseat, where she almost immediately falls asleep.

When the young man gets to the address, he finds that the girl has disappeared. There is no possible way for her to have gotten out of the car, for he has not stopped once since he picked her up, yet she is gone.

He goes up to the house, and tells his story to a middle-aged woman who answers the door. She nods sympathetically, and then tells him that the hitchhiker is the ghost of her daughter, who has been dead for ten years.

The woman explains that her daughter was killed in an automobile accident at the spot where he found her hitchhiking. She also says that other young men driving past that spot have had a similar experience.

The young man does not believe the story. The next day he goes to the cemetery to locate the girl's grave. He finds it, and there, draped over the top of the tombstone, is his jacket!

It is impossible to determine where and how this story first began. Variations of the phantom hitchhiker go back to the days of the horse and carriage. It really began to spread during the late 1940s, as the automobile became a part of almost everyone's life.

When the story is told it is usually "localized," that is it is supposed to have taken place somewhere nearby. One of the most persistent local variations is called Resurrection Mary. In this version the ghost is found hitchhiking near Resurrection Cemetery, just outside of Chicago. She is supposed to be the spirit of a girl buried in the cemetery. She was killed in an auto accident while returning from a dance at a local dance hall. She asks to be taken to the dance hall, and when the evening is over she disappears from the car of the person taking her home as the car passes Resurrection Cemetery.

In other versions the hitchhiker is a nun, or a bearded man who issues some sort of prophecy before disappearing.

# RIDE WITH THE DEAD

An Armenian tale from Turkey tells of a young man who was traveling through a part of the country with which he was not familiar. He had been badly delayed on his trip and now felt compelled to ride straight through the night.

Just as it began to get dark, he passed a cemetery and saw a young lady sitting at the roadside crying softly. He stopped his horse and asked her what was wrong. She told him that she was due in a distant town by morning, but that she was far too tired and weak to make the entire journey that night.

Since the young man happened to be going past that very town, he told the girl to climb onto his horse and that he would take her along. He had her sit in front of him so that he would be able to get a good grip on her lest she fall off.

As they rode the girl didn't say a word, and the young man noticed that she was becoming harder and harder to hold. It almost seemed as if she were getting heavier. At first he thought it was his imagination, but soon there was no mistaking it, the girl was getting heavier. He tried to stop his horse, but he couldn't.

Finally at dawn the rider reached the town that had been the girl's destination. The horse suddenly stopped of its own accord. When he dismounted and tried to help the girl down, she tumbled off the horse and sprawled on the ground. She was dead. He had ridden through the night with a corpse!

A few early risers had gathered around to watch the scene, and the young man was suddenly frightened by the thought that they would believe that he was somehow responsible for the girl's death. He tried to explain what had happened. But the onlookers didn't need any explanation.

They went on to assure him that this sort of thing had happened before. The dead girl on the ground had once lived in the village but she had been killed in a distant town some ten years past. Her family decided to bury her where she had died, but each year, on the anniversary of her death, she appeared to make an attempt to return to her native village. The villagers told the young man that the girl's relatives would be by in a short time to claim the corpse and rebury it.

# THE DEATH CAR

A popular legend particularly in the American Midwest concerns the luxury car that nobody wants.

A young couple goes to a used car lot looking for a cheap car that they can afford on their limited budget. They see an absolutely beautiful luxury car that is selling for an unbelievably low price. At first they assume that the posted price is wrong, but the salesman assures them it is correct. Then they figure there must be something seriously wrong with the car, but a test drive convinces them it is in perfect condition.

Unable to believe their luck they write a check for the car. As they drive it off the lot the salesman says enigmatically, "See you soon."

The car seems like a dream come true, for about two weeks. Then while driving in the car alone the young man notices an unpleasant smell that seems to get worse day by day. When he and his wife are in the car together, he doesn't smell a thing, so he figures it's his imagination.

Imagination or not, the smell keeps getting stronger, and when he drives alone it is almost choking, even though he has all the windows open. He examines the car from end to end. Aside from the fact that the smell seems to come from the trunk, he can't find any cause for it. He doesn't know what sort of smell it is, until one day a phrase pops into his head "the smell of death"—yes, that's what it is, the smell of death.

And then there is a new and even more ominous development. One day he glances in the rearview mirror and he sees a face. The first view is fleeting and momentary, but day by day, the face becomes clearer and more substantial. It is a heavy, brutal face. Yet when he turns around, no one is there. Still, he has the horrible feeling that one day when he turns around someone or something will be there.

As a result the young man avoids driving alone. He makes up one excuse after another. Then he notices that his wife no longer drives the car either. It is just parked most of the time.

Finally he breaks down and tells her what he has been experiencing. Her immediate reaction is relief. She has also choked on the smell, and she has seen the same brutal face.

They decide to return the car to the dealer who sold it to them. As they pull into the lot they see the same salesman. He looks as if he has been expecting them.

They offer to sell the car back to him at a loss. Then he tells them the car's history. It had once belonged to a big-time mobster, but he had double-crossed some of his associates, and they killed him. They stuffed his body in the trunk of his car and parked it in the long-term parking lot at the airport.

It was weeks before the body was discovered. Parking lot attendants became suspicious when the odor from the decomposing corpse became overpowering. The police confiscated the car. Then they had it cleaned up and sold at a police auction, where it brought a good price. But soon the new owners began complaining about the smell. Nothing they did could get rid of it. So they sold the car. The next owner had the same problem. He didn't mention the face, but he had probably seen it. He also sold the car. Each time the car was resold, it went for a lower price. And each time it was returned for the same reason.

# THE ANGELS OF MONS

No alleged ghostly event more clearly illustrates that often we see what we want to see than the incident of the Angels of Mons.

On August 23, 1917, at the start of the First World War, badly outnumbered British troops were briefly able to hold off fifty German divisions at the Battle of Mons. It was long enough to help the French army withdraw. Their bravery inspired the writer Arthur Machen to write a story called "The Bowmen," which was published in September 1917. In the story, the British soldiers facing defeat are aided by a group of phantom bowmen who fire flights of silvery arrows into the advancing Germans. Hundreds of Germans fall, and later, when their bodies are examined no wounds can be found. The story was published in the London *Evening News* on September 29.

In the autumn of 1917, when Britain was being engulfed in a tide of calamitous war news, readers seized upon this inspiring tale enthusiastically. Then something very strange began to happen. Reports began filtering back from the front that British troops actually *had* seen ghostly figures in the sky that had aided them. But in most of these reports the figures were those of angels, not medieval bowmen.

Machen immediately protested. He said he had made

the whole story up. But by that time many people didn't want to believe him. They insisted that the story was true.

And so the legend of the Angels of Mons was born.

# THE GHOSTLY TRUCK DRIVER

Throughout the United States the tale of the ghostly truck driver is told in many different versions.

This is the basic story: A young runaway is hitchhiking along an interstate. It's raining, it's cold, and he has been trying to get a ride for over two hours, without any success. Worst of all, he has no idea of where he is going, and he is very close to not caring anymore.

He hears the roar of a big eighteen-wheeler laboring up an incline. Then he sees the lights of the truck, but by this time he is just too discouraged and depressed to bother to stick out his thumb. The truck stops anyway, right alongside him. The trucker leans out of the window and says, "Where you going, kid?"

"Nowhere special," says the boy. "Just down the road."

"That's where I'm going too. Get in."

The cab of the truck is dark so the boy isn't able to get a good look at the driver. All he can tell is that the man is big and has a deep, commanding voice.

The driver begins talking, about nothing in particular. His voice inspires immediate confidence, and the boy, who is usually very distrustful and close-mouthed, finds himself telling this stranger the whole story of his unhappy life. And though he still can't see the driver's face, he knows somehow that the big man is listening closely.

Finally the truck turns into a truck stop. The driver tells the boy not to give up hope. "You're young. You've got time, and you never can tell what will happen. I've got to turn off up ahead. You get out here." The trucker shoves a ten-dollar bill into the boy's hand. "Get yourself something to eat. The food's not bad in this place, and the apple pie is terrific. Tell 'em Big Joe dropped you off. They know me, and they'll treat you right."

The boy gets out of the cab, and the rig pulls off into the darkness. In the diner the boy orders a meal, the first full meal he has had in days. Then he says to the counterman, "I'll have some apple pie. Big Joe tells me you have real good apple pie."

"You know who Big Joe is?" asks the counterman.

The boy admits that he doesn't.

Then he is told that fifteen years ago, Big Joe was driving down that stretch of road when a school bus in front of him went out of control. Joe swerved off the road to avoid the bus. Nobody on the bus was hurt, but the rig flipped over, and Big Joe was killed.

The counterman continues, "Since then, every once in a while a down-and-out hitchhiker like yourself gets picked up by Joe. He gives them a couple of bucks and drops them off here for a meal. Consider yourself lucky kid. I think he's giving you a second chance."

# A VIETNAM WAR GHOST

Many South Vietnamese soldiers were buried in the Mac Dinh Chi Cemetery just north of Saigon. On April 30, 1975, Saigon fell to the Communist victors from the North. They bulldozed the cemetery, and in the process destroyed a bronze statue called *Grief*. This was a symbol of the military cemetery. It showed a seated and exhausted soldier.

Since that time there have been rumors that passersby have reported seeing an exhausted soldier—the soldier from the statue—wandering near the ruined cemetery. The rumors indicate that the Communist authorities, fearing some sort of antigovernment provocation, or perhaps fearing the ghost itself, have sent patrols to confront it. But whenever they have approached the apparition has disappeared.

According to the *New York Times* that story has a sequel in the area north of Los Angeles called Little Saigon, where many refugees from Vietnam, including many former South Vietnamese soldiers, now live.

After the war the statue's sculptor, Nguyen Van Thu, fled to the United States. He has recreated his statue *Grief* and is hoping to place it in a cemetery where

Vietnamese residents, including many elderly veterans, will be buried.

Perhaps then the soldier's ghost will finally be put to rest.

## "I'M GOIN' HOME"

Old Zeke finally died at the age of ninety-three. Some folks said it was a blessing. Though he had enjoyed good health for most of his long life, in his last few years Zeke was terribly crippled with arthritis. For several years the best he was able to do was hobble about very painfully, unable even to straighten his back. He walked, if you can call it walking, completely bent over.

That gave the undertaker a lot of problems. Zeke's body was so badly bent, and so stiff, that he couldn't be properly laid out in his coffin. Finally the undertaker had to actually have the upper part of the body strapped down in order to get it into the coffin.

As was the custom, many of those who had known Zeke gathered at the funeral home, and sat in silence in front of the open coffin, as a sign of respect for their old, and now-departed friend.

The scene was a very quiet one for about half an hour. Then there came a squeaking and groaning sound. The coffin began to shudder. And there was a sharp report, like a pistol shot.

Zeke's body suddenly sprang up into a sitting position.

Of course, what had really happened is that the straps holding the bent old man's body down broke. When they snapped the body appeared to sit bolt upright of its own accord.

This alarming sight terrified those who had been sitting quietly in front of the coffin. Some screamed, and all rushed for the door. All except one.

Hiram, Zeke's oldest friend just sat there, with his head bowed. Then he looked up, straight at the sitting corpse.

"Zeke," he said, "If you're gettin' up, I'm goin' home."

# IF YOU DARE T...
## READ SPIN...

jf

Cohen, Daniel
AUTHOR

Screaming Skulls.
TITLE

| DATE DUE | BORROWER'S NAME |
|---|---|
| AG 19 '96 | Ashley Brant... |
| SE 3 '96 | SE 30 '96 Ashley Brait... |
| JY 21 '97 | Nicole Mansfield |
| NO 4 '97 | Rachael Grayor |
| JA 19 '98 | Dustin Erton |
| MR 15 '00 | Katie Phillips |

(pape
4-6

**HOLGATE COMMUNITY LIBRARY**
204 Railway Ave.
HOLGATE, OHIO 43527

DEMCO

# THESE FREAKS ARE FRIENDLY...
# SO JOIN THEM FOR SOME FUN

Read all the scary adventures
featuring Winston and Brock by

# DON WHITTINGTON

| | |
|---|---|
| **WEREWOLF TONIGHT** | 77513-1/$3.50 US/$4.50 Can |
| **VAMPIRE MOM** | 77936-6/$3.50 US/$4.50 Can |
| **SPOOK HOUSE** | 77937-4/$3.50 US/$4.50 Can |
| **ZOMBIE QUEEN** | 78411-4/$3.50 US/$4.99 Can |
| **FREAK SHOW** | 78412-2/$3.50 US/$4.50 Can |

*Coming Soon*

**GHOST SHIP**          78612-5/$3.50 US/$4.50 Can

---

Buy these books at your local bookstore or use this coupon for ordering:

Mail to: Avon Books, Dept BP, Box 767, Rte 2, Dresden, TN 38225                E
Please send me the book(s) I have checked above.
❏ My check or money order—no cash or CODs please—for $_____ is enclosed (please add $1.50 per order to cover postage and handling—Canadian residents add 7% GST).
❏ Charge my VISA/MC Acct#_____ Exp Date_____
Minimum credit card order is two books or $7.50 (please add postage and handling charge of $1.50 per order—Canadian residents add 7% GST). For faster service, call 1-800-762-0779. Residents of Tennessee, please call 1-800-633-1607. Prices and numbers are subject to change without notice. Please allow six to eight weeks for delivery.

Name_____
Address_____
City_____State/Zip_____
Telephone No._____                          DW 0796

# Join in the Wild and Crazy Adventures with Some Trouble-Making Plants

## by Nancy McArthur

**THE PLANT THAT ATE DIRTY SOCKS**
75493-2/ $3.99 US/ $5.50 Can

**THE RETURN OF THE PLANT THAT ATE DIRTY SOCKS**
75873-3/ $3.99 US/ $5.50 Can

**THE ESCAPE OF THE PLANT THAT ATE DIRTY SOCKS**
76756-2/ $3.50 US/ $4.25 Can

**THE SECRET OF THE PLANT THAT ATE DIRTY SOCKS**
76757-0/ $3.50 US/ $4.50 Can

**MORE ADVENTURES OF THE PLANT THAT ATE DIRTY SOCKS**
77663-4/ $3.50 US/ $4.50 Can

**THE PLANT THAT ATE DIRTY SOCKS GOES UP IN SPACE**
77664-2/ $3.99 US/ $5.50 Can

**THE MYSTERY OF THE PLANT THAT ATE DIRTY SOCKS**
78318-5/ $3.99 US/ $4.99 Can

---

Buy these books at your local bookstore or use this coupon for ordering:

Mail to: Avon Books, Dept BP, Box 767, Rte 2, Dresden, TN 38225      E
Please send me the book(s) I have checked above.
❏ My check or money order—no cash or CODs please—for $_____ is enclosed (please add $1.50 per order to cover postage and handling—Canadian residents add 7% GST).
❏ Charge my VISA/MC Acct#_____ Exp Date_____
Minimum credit card order is two books or $7.50 (please add postage and handling charge of $1.50 per order—Canadian residents add 7% GST). For faster service, call 1-800-762-0779. Residents of Tennessee, please call 1-800-633-1607. Prices and numbers are subject to change without notice. Please allow six to eight weeks for delivery.

Name_____
Address_____
City_____ State/Zip_____
Telephone No._____      ESC 0396

# Avon Camelot Presents
# Award-Winning Author

# THEODORE TAYLOR

**THE CAY**                  00142-X $4.50 US/$6.50 Can

After being blinded in a fatal shipwreck, Phillip was rescued from the shark-infested waters by the kindly old black man who had worked on deck. Cast up on a remote island, together they began an amazing adventure.

**TIMOTHY OF THE CAY**

72522-3 $3.99 US/$4.99 Can

The stunning prequel-sequel to *The Cay*.

**THE TROUBLE WITH TUCK**

62711-6/ $4.50 US/$6.50 Can

**TUCK TRIUMPHANT**    71323-3/ $3.99 US/$4.99 Can

**MARIA**                  72120-1/ $3.99 US/ $4.99 Can

**THE MALDONADO MIRACLE**

70023-9/$3.99 US/$4.99 Can

---

Buy these books at your local bookstore or use this coupon for ordering:

Mail to: Avon Books, Dept BP, Box 767, Rte 2, Dresden, TN 38225          E
Please send me the book(s) I have checked above.
❏ My check or money order—no cash or CODs please—for $_____ is enclosed (please add $1.50 per order to cover postage and handling—Canadian residents add 7% GST).
❏ Charge my VISA/MC Acct#_____Exp Date_____
Minimum credit card order is two books or $7.50 (please add postage and handling charge of $1.50 per order—Canadian residents add 7% GST). For faster service, call 1-800-762-0779. Residents of Tennessee, please call 1-800-633-1607. Prices and numbers are subject to change without notice. Please allow six to eight weeks for delivery.

Name_____
Address_____
City_____State/Zip_____
Telephone No._____          TAY 1095

# From out of the Shadows...
## Stories Filled with Mystery and Suspense by
# MARY DOWNING HAHN

**TIME FOR ANDREW**
72469-3/$4.50 US/$6.50 Can

**DAPHNE'S BOOK**
72355-7/$4.50 US/$6.50 Can

**THE TIME OF THE WITCH**
71116-8/ $3.99 US/ $4.99 Can

**STEPPING ON THE CRACKS**
71900-2/ $3.99 US/ $4.99 Can

**THE DEAD MAN IN INDIAN CREEK**
71362-4/ $4.50 US/ $5.99 Can

**THE DOLL IN THE GARDEN**
70865-5/ $4.50 US/ $6.50 Can

**FOLLOWING THE MYSTERY MAN**
70677-6/ $3.99 US/ $4.99 Can

**TALLAHASSEE HIGGINS**
70500-1/ $3.99 US/ $4.99 Can

**WAIT TILL HELEN COMES**
70442-0/ $3.99 US/ $5.50 Can

**THE SPANISH KIDNAPPING DISASTER**
71712-3/ $3.99 US/ $4.99 Can

**THE JELLYFISH SEASON**
71635-6/ $3.99 US/ $5.50 Can

**THE SARA SUMMER**
72354-9/ $3.99 US/ $4.99 Can

---

Buy these books at your local bookstore or use this coupon for ordering:

Mail to: Avon Books, Dept BP, Box 767, Rte 2, Dresden, TN 38225      E
Please send me the book(s) I have checked above.
❏ My check or money order—no cash or CODs please—for $_____ is enclosed (please add $1.50 per order to cover postage and handling—Canadian residents add 7% GST).
❏ Charge my VISA/MC Acct#_____ Exp Date_____
Minimum credit card order is two books or $7.50 (please add postage and handling charge of $1.50 per order—Canadian residents add 7% GST). For faster service, call 1-800-762-0779. Residents of Tennessee, please call 1-800-633-1607. Prices and numbers are subject to change without notice. Please allow six to eight weeks for delivery.

Name_____
Address_____
City_____ State/Zip_____
Telephone No._____      MDH 0396